H. W. BRANDS'S

AMERICAN PORTRAITS

The big stories of history unfold over decades and touch millions of lives; telling them can require books of several hundred pages. But history has other stories, smaller tales that center on individual men and women at particular moments that can peculiarly illuminate history's grand sweep. These smaller stories are the subjects of American Portraits: tightly written, vividly rendered accounts of lost or forgotten lives and crucial historical moments.

H. W. BRANDS

THE HEARTBREAK OF
$\mathcal{A}$ARON $\mathcal{B}$URR

H. W. Brands is the Dickson Allen Anderson Professor of History at the University of Texas at Austin. He was a finalist for the Pulitzer Prize in biography for *The First American: The Life and Times of Benjamin Franklin* and for *Traitor to His Class: The Privileged Life and Radical Presidency of Franklin Delano Roosevelt.*

www.hwbrands.com

ALSO BY H. W. BRANDS

The Reckless Decade

T.R.

The First American

The Age of Gold

Lone Star Nation

Andrew Jackson

Traitor to His Class

*The Murder of Jim Fisk
for the Love of Josie Mansfield*

American Colossus

THE

HEARTBREAK

OF

AARON

BURR

THE

HEARTBREAK

OF

Aaron Burr

AMERICAN PORTRAITS

H. W. BRANDS

ANCHOR BOOKS

A Division of Random House, Inc.
New York

AN ANCHOR BOOKS ORIGINAL, MAY 2012

Illustrations credits: Wikimedia Commons: p. 1;
New-York Historical Society: p. 2; New York Public
Library: pp. 3 and 4; National Archives: p. 4; Library
of Congress: pp. 5 (top), 6, 7 (top), 8; Independence
National Historical Park: p. 7 (bottom).

Library of Congress Cataloging-in-Publication Data
Brands, H. W.
The heartbreak of Aaron Burr / H. W. Brands.
p. cm.—(American portraits)
ISBN 978-0-307-74326-8 (pbk.)
1. Burr, Aaron, 1756–1836.   2. Statesman—United States—
Biography.   3. Vice-Presidents—United States—Biography.
4. Soldiers—United States—Biography.   5. United States—
History—Revolution, 1775–1783—Biography.   6. United
States—Politics and government—1783–1865.   I. Title.
E302.6.B9B73 2012
973.4'6092—dc23
[B] 2011044372

Author photograph © Marsha Miller
Book design by Rebecca Aidlin
Cover design by W. Staehle
Front cover drawing: Hulton Archive/Getty Images

www.anchorbooks.com

Printed in the United States of America
10 9 8 7 6 5 4 3 2 1

THE

HEARTBREAK

OF

AARON

BURR

I

———

"Patience, my dear children, and you shall hear all."

The old man sits at a cramped table in a spare room overlooking a narrow street in lower [downtown] Manhattan. He writes clearly but swiftly, in the practiced hand of one who has written much in the course of an accomplished life conducted often on the run.

He tells his daughter and her son of his recent arrival from abroad. "The ebb carried us up to [movement of tide] Riker's Island, one mile from Hell Gate, and here, being met by the flood, we [NY main jail] cast anchor to wait for the ebb, which would make at half past seven. In the meantime came up a breeze from S.E. Nothing could have more perfectly accorded with my wishes, as we must now necessarily arrive in New York about ten in the evening."

The old man's absence from his home city has been forced, and he fears retribution from the law, which is why he hoped to arrive after nightfall. "However, as the hour approached, the captain began to doubt whether it would not be too dark to go through Hell Gate, and thought it would be more prudent to wait till morning. I combated this childish apprehension, but without effect."

He sought another vessel to complete his journey. "There hove in sight a very small sailboat, standing down." He paid two men to row him over. "The sailboat proved to be a pleasure boat belonging to two young farmers of Long Island. They were not bound to New York but to the Narrows, but very kindly agreed to put me on shore in the city." The wind failed, though, and the sailboat succumbed to the seaward pull of the tide. "It seemed inevitable that I must make a voyage to the Narrows." But luck, in the form of another vessel, intervened again. "When we were nearly opposite the Battery I heard the noise of oars, and hailed, was answered, and I begged them to come alongside. It proved to be two vagabonds in a skiff, probably on some thieving voyage. They were very happy to set me on shore in the city for a dollar, and at half past eleven I was landed."

He recalled the Water Street address of a trusted friend. A decade earlier he had counted many friends in New York and many more admirers across America. But nearly all had abandoned him. Many thought him dead; not a few wished him so. Yet his friend in Water Street remained. "Thither I went cheerfully, and rejoicing in my good fortune." The rejoicing soon ended. "I knocked and knocked, but no answer. I knocked still harder, supposing they were asleep, till one of the neighbors opened a window and told me that nobody lived there."

The news was sobering, perhaps fatal. Was there no one in the city who would take him in? A murder charge looms over his head; after all he has risked to return home, to see his beloved daughter and darling grandson, will he face instead the sheriff and the hangman? He considered his options. "To walk about the whole night would be too fatiguing. To have sat and slept on any stoop would have been no hardship"—he had suffered much worse during his exile—"but, then, the danger that the first watchman who might pass would take me up as a vagrant and carry me to the watchhouse was a denouement not at all to my mind."

He paced the sidewalks for an hour. He saw a lamp in a house fronting an alley. The house looked disreputable and consequently, under his peculiar circumstances, comparatively safe. He woke the owner and asked if he might sleep there the rest of the night. He was led to a small garret where five men were snoring. "I threw open the window to have air, lay down, and slept profoundly till six."

He paid his host twelve cents for the floor space and reentered the alley. He returned to Water Street, for lack of a better idea, and was greatly relieved to discover that the neighbor was wrong; his friend still lived there. He had merely been gone awhile. The friend greeted him warmly but cautiously. He said he could not stay in that house but might lodge briefly with his brother, Sam, in a house around the corner.

"And here I am," the old man writes his daughter, "in possession of Sam's room in Stone Street, in the city of New York, on this eighth day of June, anno domini 1812, just four years since we parted at this very place."

2

Aaron Burr's great love begins amid the violence and confusion of the Revolutionary War. He is a colonel in the Continental Army; she, the widow of a British officer killed in the West Indies. He encounters Theodosia while protecting her home from American raiders who impute the Toryism of the deceased to his widow. She admires the dark-eyed, black-haired young officer, a common reaction among Burr's female acquaintances. Less predictable is the affection *he* develops toward *her*. She is ten years his elder and neither beautiful nor rich. But she *is* intelligent, educated and willing to speak her mind. The women Burr grew up among were sometimes intelligent and often out-. spoken, but none had much education or seemed to miss it. Burr is fascinated by this woman with whom he can converse as an equal.

A battle injury compels him to retire from the army and frees him to court Theodosia. They marry in 1782. She gives him a daughter, whom he names after her. He promises to provide the younger Theodosia all the advantages of education and expectation the well-to-do typically accord their male children but deny their girls. "If I could foresee that Theo would become a *mere* fashionable woman," he tells her mother, "with all the attendant frivolity and vacuity of mind, adorned with whatever grace and allurement, I would earnestly pray God to take her forthwith hence. But I yet hope, by her, to convince the world what neither sex appear to believe: that women have *souls!*"

Theo idolizes her father from the moment she can express herself. "She frequently talks of, and calls on, her dear papa," her mother writes Burr when the child is two and he is away. "Your dear Theodosia cannot hear you spoken of without an apparent melancholy; insomuch that her nurse is obliged to exert her invention to divert her, and myself avoid to mention you in her presence. She was one whole day indifferent to everything but your name. Her attachment is not of a common nature."

Others will note the uncommon nature of the attachment between father and daughter, which grows only stronger with time. Burr directs Theo's education from his library when at home and from his stagecoach, his hotel and wherever his law practice takes him when he is traveling. "It is surprising that you tell me nothing of Theo," he chides his wife when Theo is seven. "I would by no means have her writing and arithmetic neglected. It is the part of her education which is of the most present importance. If Shepherd"—one of her tutors—"will not attend her in the house, another must be had; but I had rather pay him double than employ another."

Theo's mother endorses the educational project, within the limits of maternal tenderness. "She begins to cipher," she assures her husband regarding Theo's arithmetic studies. French proceeds apace. "Mr. Chevalier attends regularly, and I take care she never omits learning her French lesson. I believe she makes most progress in this." Music lessons pose a logistical challenge. "She must either have a forte-piano at home, or renounce learning it."

Theo responds with spirit, including resistance to excessive study. "I will not use severity; and without it, at present, I can obtain nothing," her mother writes Burr when Theo is being stubborn, albeit charmingly so. "The moment we are alone, she tries to amuse me with her improvement, which the little jade knows will always command my attention." Theo doesn't write her father as frequently as he wishes. "Theo has begun to write several letters, but never finished one," her mother explains. "The only time she has to write is also the hour of general leisure, and, when once she is interrupted, there is no making her return to work."

Burr wants Theo to learn to ride horseback; her mother reminds him that the day is only so long. "She writes and ciphers from five in the morning to eight, and also the same hours in the evening. This prevents our riding at those hours, except Saturday and Sunday; otherwise I should cheerfully follow your directions."

The paternal encouragement pays off. "Theo makes amazing progress at figures," her mother reports. "Though Louisa"—an older girl—"has worked at them all winter, and appeared quite an adept at first, yet Theo is now before her, and assists her to make her sums. You will really be surprised at her improvement."

For reward the mother takes her daughter and some friends for a ride in the country. "We have a good plain Dutch wagon, that I prefer to a carriage when at Pelham, as the exercise is much better. We ride in numbers and are well jolted, and without dread. 'Tis the most powerful exercise I know. No spring seats, but, like so many pigs, we bundle together on straw. Four miles are equal to twenty. . . . I hope you will see our little girl rosy cheeked and plump as a partridge."

3

"*I was acquainted with Burr, and I thought well acquainted* with him, when in the height of his power and fame," Erastus Root will remember. Root meets Burr in the courtroom, and also Alexander Hamilton, the other standout of the New York bar. "As a lawyer and as a scholar he was not inferior to Hamilton. His reasoning powers were at least equal. Their *modes* of argument were very different. Hamilton was very diffuse and wordy. His words were so well chosen, and his sentences so finely formed into a swelling current, that the hearer would be captivated. The listener would admire if he was not convinced. Burr's arguments were generally methodized and compact. I used to say of them, when they were rivals at the bar, that Burr would say as much in half an hour as Hamilton in two hours. Burr was terse and convincing, while Hamilton was flowing and rapturous. They were much the greatest men in this state, and perhaps the greatest men in the United States."

When he isn't directing Theo's education, Burr constructs a career as a lawyer and a politician. His intellectual and rhetorical gifts serve him in both arenas. He settles in New York after the Revolution and commences a law practice that wins him friends, influence and sufficient income to buy a handsome estate, Richmond Hill, overlooking the Hudson two miles above the tip of Manhattan. He fills one of the finest libraries in the city with the latest editions from London and the European continent, and he entertains distinguished visitors from several states as well as philosophers and aristocrats from abroad. Because he never counts costs, his purchases outrun his income, and, barely noticing it, he falls behind with his creditors. Yet they assume that his earning power will continue to grow and gladly lend him more.

Easy credit simultaneously assists the political career Burr is building. He serves in the state assembly and as attorney general before seeking election as one of New York's two senators to the freshly reconfigured federal government. His opponent, Philip Schuyler, would have made a distinguished statesman in the days of Rome, being august in demeanor and imperious in manner, but he lacks the popular touch increasingly required in the politics of republican America. More to the point, he has enemies in the New York legislature, which will choose to retain or replace him. It doesn't help his chances that his son-in-law and ally, Alexander Hamilton, widely thought the genius behind President George Washington, is even haughtier and, in some quarters, more thoroughly disliked.

Burr's many gifts include a talent for ingratiating: he can cause the most diverse, insightful people to think him a fine, capable fellow. He persuades the New York legislators to select him over Schuyler—and thereby over Hamilton. Schuyler accepts the defeat with comparative grace, but Hamilton takes the verdict both personally and politically. Burr's victory insults Hamilton's family, and it threatens the congressional majority Hamilton requires to effect his ambitions as Treasury secretary. An associate tells Hamilton of a "passionate courtship" between his principal rivals, Thomas Jefferson and James Madison, and Burr. "Delenda est Carthago"—Carthage must be destroyed: the refrain of the Roman intransigent Cato— "I suppose is the maxim adopted with respect to you," Hamilton's man says of the enmity he perceives in Jefferson, Madison and now Burr toward Hamilton.

In the first decade of the federal republic, political parties begin to form. The framers of the Constitution neither expected parties nor much liked them. Most anticipated a high-minded politics in which the nation's eminent men, knowing one another and bound by mutual respect and shared devotion to the common weal, would debate policy on its merits. But the patriotic glue of the Revolutionary War wears off, and new men enter the arena. Predispositions toward government emerge; around the predispositions, factions develop; the factions become parties. Jefferson and Madison head one party, the Republicans, which professes opposition to an energetic central government. Hamilton and John Adams head the other, the Federalists, which deems energy essential in government. George Washington attaches to neither party but leans Federalist.

Jefferson's Republicans see Burr as useful in probing the weakness of Hamilton's Federalists in Hamilton's home state. Building up Burr will force Hamilton to defend his New York political base and will distract him from the broader objects of his policy ambitions.

A Republican connection serves Burr's own purposes. Burr's grandfather Jonathan Edwards, the famous Calvinist minister, was the most eminent theologian in America; Burr's father, Aaron Burr, president of the College of New Jersey at Princeton, was the country's foremost educator. Burr, who precociously graduated from Princeton at the age of sixteen and started at once on a professional path in law, sees no reason he should not become America's greatest political figure. George Washington enjoys a preeminence no contemporary can match, and Jefferson and Adams rank just below Washington. But after them, who will guide the country? Burr considers himself as capable as Hamilton and Madison and at least as clever. Why should he not become president one day?

He mustn't tip his hand too soon, though. He shares his thoughts with his wife but no one else. When they are together they speak in confidence; when they are apart he writes in cipher, knowing that postmasters—appointed by Hamilton's Federalist party—aren't above opening letters sent by persons in whom their sponsors take interest. The coding is simple, primarily substituting numbers for names. But it serves its purpose for Burr. And it makes Hamilton, who learns that his rival has something to hide, distrust him the more.

4

The seat of the new government is Philadelphia, to which Burr travels during the congressional terms. He becomes a Senate figure valued by his Republican allies and feared by his Federalist foes. His watch-work mind masters the art of parliamentary maneuver; his succinct speech bolsters the measures he favors and skewers the ones he opposes. His prospects prosper and seem likely, perhaps before long, to approach his ambitions.

Yet he never lacks time for Theo. "Enclosed in Bartow's last letter came one which, from the handwriting, I supposed to be from that great fat fellow, Colonel Troup," he writes her not long before her tenth Christmas. "Judge of my pleasure and surprise when I opened and found it was from my dear little girl. You improve much in your writing. Let your next be in small hand." And let it be soon, for Theo continues to write less often than her father desires. "Why do you neither acknowledge nor answer my last letter? That is not kind—it is scarcely civil. I beg you will not take a fortnight to answer this, as you did the other. . . . I love to hear from you, and still more to receive your letters."

He buys her presents. "I rose up suddenly from the sofa," he writes one evening, "and rubbing my head—'What book shall I buy for her?' said I to myself, 'She reads so much and so rapidly that it is not easy to find proper and amusing French books for her; and yet I am so flattered with her progress in that language that I am resolved that she shall, at all events, be gratified. Indeed, I owe it to her.' So, after walking once or twice briskly across the floor, I took my hat and sallied out, determined not to return till I had purchased something. It was not my first attempt. I went into one bookseller's shop after another. I found plenty of fairy tales and such nonsense, fit for the generality of children of nine or ten years old. 'These,' said I, 'will never do. Her understanding begins to be above such things.' But I could see nothing that I would offer with pleasure to *an intelligent, well-informed girl of nine years old.* I began to be discouraged. The hour of dining was come. 'But I will search a little longer.' I persevered. At last I found it. I found the very thing I sought. It is contained in two volumes octavo, handsomely bound, and with prints and registers. It is a work of fancy, but replete with instruction and amusement." He has planned to mail it but changes his mind. "I must present it with my own hand."

He flatters Theo with the importance he places on their correspondence. "In looking over a list made yesterday (and now before me) of letters of consequence to be answered immediately, I find the name of T. Burr," he writes. "At the time I made the memorandum I did not advert to the compliment I paid you by putting your name in a list with some of the most eminent persons in the

United States." Her most recent letter, written in French, is her most accomplished yet. "If the whole performance was your own, which I am inclined to hope and believe, it indicates an improvement in style, in knowledge of the French, and in your handwriting. I have therefore not only read it several times, but shown it to several persons with pride and pleasure."

Theo's progress confirms his views of the potential of women. He encounters a new book by Mary Wollstonecraft, a British philosopher and educator, called *A Vindication of the Rights of Woman*. "I had heard it spoken of with a coldness little calculated to excite attention," he explains to Theo's mother. "But as I read with avidity and prepossession everything written by a lady, I made haste to procure it, and spent the last night, almost the whole of it, in reading it. Be assured that your sex has in *her* an able advocate. It is, in my opinion, a work of genius. She has successfully adopted the style of Rousseau's *Emilius;* and her comment on that work, especially what relates to female education, contains more good sense than all the other criticisms upon him which I have seen put together. I promise myself much pleasure in reading it to you." He laments that the book has won little audience in America. "Is it owing to ignorance or prejudice that I have not yet met a single person who had discovered or would allow the merit of this work?"

Burr credits his wife as well for his appreciation of women's abilities. "It was a knowledge of your mind which first inspired me with a respect for that of your sex," he writes the elder Theodosia. "And with some regret I con-fess that the ideas which you have often heard me express in favor of female intellectual powers are founded on what I have imagined, more than what I have seen, except in you." He ponders why others have not allowed women to advance. "I have endeavored to trace the causes of this *rare* display of genius in women, and find them in the errors of education, of prejudice, and of habit. I admit that men are equally, nay more, much more to blame than women. Boys and girls are generally educated much in the same way till they are eight or nine years of age, and it is admitted that girls make at least equal progress with the boys; generally, indeed, they make better. Why, then, has it never been thought worth the attempt to discover, by fair experiment, the particular age at which the male superiority becomes so evident?"

Theo becomes Burr's experiment. He is never less than loving toward her, but he is frequently insistent. "I have a thousand questions to ask, my dear Theo, but nothing to communicate," he writes from Philadelphia. "And thus I fear it will be throughout the winter, for my time is con-sumed in the dull uniformity of study and attendance in Senate. But every hour of *your* day is interesting to me. I would give—what would I *not* give?—to see or know even your most trifling actions and amusements. This, how-ever, is more than I can ask or expect. But I do expect with impatience your journal. Ten minutes every evening I demand; if you should choose to make it twenty, I shall be the better pleased. You are to note the occurrences of the day as concisely as you can; and, at your pleasure, to add any short reflections or remarks that may arise." He furnishes a sample for her to emulate, with entries inspired by her current studies:

16th December, 1793.

Learned 230 lines, which finished Horace. Heigh-ho for Terence and the Greek grammar to-morrow.

Practised two hours less thirty-five minutes, which I begged off.

Hewlett (dancing-master) did not come.

Began Gibbon last evening. I find he requires as much study and attention as Horace; so I shall not rank the reading of *him* among amusements.

Skated an hour; fell twenty times, and find the advantage of a hard head.

Ma better—dined with us at table, and is still sitting up and free from pain.

5

He hopes *Theo's ma will be free from pain.* Theodosia's health has taken a mysterious turn; her appetite is failing and her strength flagging for reasons her doctors at first cannot fathom. Benjamin Rush of Philadelphia is the most distinguished physician in America and a family friend; Burr asks him to consult on the case. Rush prescribes various medications. When the symptoms defy his treatment and simply grow worse, he concludes that the malady is cancer. Medicine might ease Theodosia's pain but it cannot halt her condition's grim advance.

"The account of your mamma's health distresses me extremely," Burr writes Theo. "If she does not get better soon, I will quit Congress altogether and go home." Theodosia is too ill to write, as Burr reminds their daughter. "My last letter to you was almost an angry one, at which you cannot be much surprised when you recollect the length of time of your silence, and that you are my only correspondent respecting the concerns of the family."

Burr tries to ease his daughter's fears for her mother by casting Theo's reports on Theodosia's condition as material for further education. "When your letters are written with tolerable spirit and correctness, I read them two or three times before I perceive any fault in them, being wholly engaged with the pleasure they afford me," he tells Theo. "But for your sake, it is necessary that I should also peruse them with an eye of criticism. The following are the only misspelled words. You write *acurate* for *accurate; laudnam* for *laudanum; intirely* for *entirely*. This last word, indeed, is spelled both ways, but *entirely* is the most usual and the most proper. Continue to use all these words in your next letter, that I may see that you know the true spelling. And tell me what is laudanum? Where and how made? And what are its effects?" He quotes and comments on a sentence Theo has written about a particular form of treatment: "'It was what she had long wished for, and was at a loss how to procure *it*.' Don't you see that this sentence would have been perfect and much more elegant without the last *it*?"

Yet he cannot hide his own concern for his wife. "I am extremely impatient for your farther account of mamma's health," he writes Theo. "The necessity of laudanum twice a day is a very disagreeable and alarming circumstance. Your letter was written a week ago, since which I have no account."

He explains that he is importuning Dr. Rush, to modest avail. "He enumerates over to me all the articles which have been repeatedly tried, and some of which did never agree with your mamma. He is, however, particularly desirous that she should again try milk—a spoonful only at a time: another attempt, he thinks, should be made with porter, in some shape or other. Sweet oil, molasses, and milk, in equal proportions, he has known to agree with stomachs which had rejected everything else. Yet he says, and with show of reason, that these things depend so much on the taste, the habits of life, the peculiarity of constitution, that she and her attending physician can be the best, if not the only advisers." Still, Burr insists that his friend prescribe, and Rush accedes. "Doctor Rush says that he cannot conceive animal food to be particularly necessary; nourishment is the great object. He approves much of the milk punch and chocolate. The stomach must on no account be offended. The intermission of the pills for a few days (not however for a whole week) he thinks not amiss to aid in determining its effects. The quantity may yet be increased without danger, but the present dose is in his opinion sufficient; but after some days continual use, a small increase might be useful."

A week of this course produces another recommendation from Rush—and another chance for Burr to distract his daughter with a lesson. "Doctor Rush thinks that bark would not be amiss, but may be beneficial if the stomach does not rebuke it, which must be constantly the first object of attention. He recommends either the cold infusion or substance as least likely to offend the stomach. Be able, upon my arrival, to tell me the difference between an *infusion* and *decoction;* and the history, the virtues, and the botanical or medical name of the bark."

The treatments fail to stem the cancer. Theodosia's last

days are agonizing for her and excruciating for her husband and daughter. Burr and Theo comfort each other; the experience binds the thirty-eight-year-old widower and the eleven-year-old girl more tightly than ever. Each is all the other has left of the one they have lost. "The mother of my Theo was the best woman and finest lady I have ever known," Burr sadly observes.

6

The loss of her mother compels Theo to mature more rapidly than ever. Her father treats her almost as an adult, sharing his experiences in person when he can and by letter when he is gone. "We arrived here yesterday, after a hot, tedious passage of seven days," he explains amid a journey to Albany in the summer of 1794. "We were delayed as well by accidents as by calms and contrary winds. The first evening, being under full sail"—packet boats ply the Hudson in the era before railroads—"we ran ashore at Tappan, and lay there aground, in a very uncomfortable situation, twenty-four hours. With great labor and fatigue we got off on the following night, and had scarce got under sail before we missed our longboat. We lost the whole tide in hunting for it, and so lay till the morning of Wednesday. Having then made sail again, with a pretty strong head wind, at the very first tack the Dutch horse fell overboard. The poor devil was at the time tied about the neck with a rope, so that he seemed to have only the alternatives of hanging or drowning (for the river is here about four miles wide, and the water was very rough); fortunately for him, the rope broke, and he went souse into the water. His weight sunk him so deep that we were at least fifty yards from him before he came up. He snorted off the water, and turning round once or twice, as if to see where he was, then recollecting the way to New York, he immediately swam off down the river with all force. We fitted out our longboat in pursuit of him, and at length drove him on shore on the Westchester side, where I hired a man to take him to Frederick's. All this delayed us nearly a whole tide more. The residue of the voyage was without accident, except such as you may picture to yourself in a small cabin, with seven men, seven women, and two crying children—two of the women being the most splenetic, ill-humored animals you can imagine."

Senate business subsequently takes Burr to Washington, the federal city rising on the banks of the Potomac. "Since Tuesday last I have been here much against my will; arrested by high command; performing quarantine by authority not to be questioned or controverted," he writes Theo. "In plain English, I am sick. On Wednesday I found one side of my face as large as your uncle F.'s; red swollen eyes; ears buzzing and almost stopped; throat so closed as to refuse a passage to words out or food in; and a stupid mazy-headedness, well adapted to the brilliancy of my figure. Being the guest of my friends Law and Duncanson, I receive from them the most distressing attentions, but especially from Miss Duncanson, a well-bred, sprightly, and agreeable woman. My person had not, however, till this morning, received its last embellishment. Alexis came in at his usual hour, and presenting himself at my bedside, after staring at me for half a minute, exclaimed, with an air of great astonishment: *Diable!* And not a word more. *Qu'a-t-il, Alexis?* To which he made not a word of reply, but fell to drawing up the curtains; and having also very deliberately opened the window-shutters, he returned again to his examination. After gazing for some time (which I found it useless to interrupt), he *diabled* two or three times at intervals of some seconds, and then pronounced that I had *ou la petite vérole ou la rougeole;* and to convince me, brought a glass. In truth he did not *diable* without reason, for my whole face, neck, hands, and arms are most bountifully covered with something like the measles or rash."

Theo becomes the mistress of Richmond Hill. She greets guests at Burr's side and manages the estate in his absence. "By this post I received a letter from Colonel Ward, requesting leave to remove his family into my house," Burr writes her from Philadelphia. "He lives, you may recollect, in the part of the town which is said to be sickly. I could not therefore refuse. He will call on you to go out with him. You had better, immediately on receipt of this, go out yourself and apprize Anthony and Peggy"— the heads of the household staff.

Theo's social triumph occurs in her fifteenth year, when her father is in Philadelphia. Joseph Brant is a Mohawk chief who sided with the British during the Revolutionary War but went on to make himself indispensable to President Washington in the latter's attempts to pacify the frontier. On periodic visits to Philadelphia, Brant is feted as the noblest of savages: a child of the forest equally at home in the salons of the capital. Burr befriends him and urges him to stop at Richmond Hill on his return to the wilderness. He supplies a letter of introduction to Theo: "This will be handed to you by Colonel Brant, the celebrated Indian Chief. He is a man of education—speaks and writes English perfectly—and has seen much of Europe and America. Receive him with respect and hospitality."

Theo complies, hosting an elaborate dinner for Brant. The leading men of the city bring their ladies; all are impressed by the Mohawk's intelligence and demeanor and by Theo's confidence and self-command. Her performance evokes many months of admiring comment, with the congratulations aimed equally at the remarkable daughter and the father who is rearing her to be such an accomplished woman.

7

Burr resumes his residency in New York after his Senate term ends in 1797. Besides allowing him more time with Theo, the move enables him to devote his attention to New York politics, which, he recognizes, must be his path to higher office. The Federalists control the states east of New York, the Republicans those to New York's south and west; New York itself holds the balance in the country as a whole. And in New York the Federalists and Republicans are closely matched, with Hamilton heading the former and Burr the latter. Hamilton employs his formidable intelligence and powerful persuasive skills on behalf of the Federalist ticket for the New York legislature, which will choose not only New York's senators but also the state's electors in the 1800 presidential contest. Burr counters with assiduous organization and subtle arguments in the most telling places. When the votes are counted, Burr and the Republicans win a narrow but decisive victory.

The news travels from New York to Philadelphia as fast as swift horses can gallop. Jefferson, the Republican vice president and candidate for president, is accosted by

Adams, the Federalist president and likewise candidate for president. "I understand that you are to beat me in this contest," Adams grumbles to Jefferson, referring to the New York results and their consequences for the national contest.

"Mr. Adams," Jefferson responds, "this is no personal contest between you and me. Two systems of principles, on the subject of government, divide our fellow citizens into two parties. With one of these you concur, and I with the other. As we have been longer on the public stage than most of those now living, our names happen to be more generally known. One of these parties, therefore, has put your name at its head, the other mine. Were we both to die today, tomorrow two other names would be in the place of ours, without any change in the motion of the machinery."

Adams takes little comfort from Jefferson's philosophizing; Hamilton takes none at all. Hamilton tries to reverse the effect of the New York vote by lobbying the legislature to change the rules for choosing the state's presidential electors. Jefferson, learning what is afoot, calls on Burr to guarantee the result and with it the election.

Burr blocks Hamilton's effort, saving the day for the Republicans and further aggrieving Hamilton, who, realizing he cannot touch Jefferson or Burr, perversely vents his rage on Adams. Hamilton has never liked or respected Adams; he now composes a pamphlet explaining why. He intends for the pamphlet to be circulated privately among Federalists, as a means of shifting the party away from

Adams. But Burr's agents procure a copy and arrange the public airing of its most damaging passages. Hamilton's exposed sabotage sends the Federalists into an uproar and kills what small hopes Adams has retained of being returned to office. The only thing left is the formality of casting the votes for Jefferson.

The Constitution, however, clouds the formality. It specifies that each elector will cast two votes, the candidate with the most votes becoming president, the runner-up vice president. Jefferson, the Republican leader in a contest already secured to the Republican party, expects an easy victory. The Republican members of Congress intend Burr to become vice president in recognition of his good work against Hamilton and in anticipation of similar service in the future. The Republicans' strategy is to have one of their electors withhold his second vote, giving Jefferson the presidency and Burr the vice presidency.

But confusion fouls the implementation, and Jefferson and Burr finish in a tie, with 73 electors each. This throws the race into the House of Representatives and the parties into a muddle. The Federalists still control the House, where they can determine which Republican—Jefferson or Burr—will become the next president. Most fear Jefferson more than Burr, and some are tempted to tip the election Burr's way.

Federalists and Republicans recognize that the fate of the nascent republic hangs in the balance. For the first time the American political system is being asked to transfer power from one party to the other. If it can manage the transfer, the prospects for successful self-government in America will improve dramatically. If it can't, they will plummet—and perhaps plunge the country into the kind of civil strife European skeptics have consistently predicted for the upstart republic.

Burr appreciates the stakes and distances himself from any effort to overrule the obvious will of the people. He tells a Republican member of the House that he doesn't believe the Federalists will be so base as actually to vote for him over Jefferson. "As to my friends," he continues, "they would dishonor my views and insult my feelings by a suspicion that I would submit to be instrumental in counteracting the wishes and expectations of the United States. And I now constitute you my proxy to declare these sentiments if the occasion should require."

The Federalists aren't listening to Burr. They consult instead their own judgment as to what will cause the most mischief for the Republicans. Some dream that Burr might be won to the Federalist side. Hamilton bitterly warns them off. "It is a vain hope," he writes to a Federalist ally. "To accomplish his ends, he must lean upon unprincipled men, and will continue to adhere to myrmidons who have hitherto surrounded him. To these he will no doubt add able rogues of the Federal party but he will employ the rogues of all parties to overrule the good men of all parties, and to prosecute projects which wise men of every description will disapprove." To conspire with Burr will ruin what remains of the Federalists' future. "He is too cold-blooded and too determined a conspirator ever to change his plan. . . . Adieu to the Federal Troy if they once introduce this Grecian horse into their citadel."

Hamilton's warning quells the spoiling mood among the Federalists, who concede Jefferson the victory the electors have intended to give him. Burr accepts the vice presidency with appropriate grace but remembers Hamilton's malign remarks.

8

―――――

Amid the controversy Theo marries. Her intelligence and accomplishments don't exempt her from the constraints of the common-law tradition that a woman's legal existence derives from that of the most significant male in her life: her father, her husband, her eldest son. Theo is too independent-minded to remain the ward of her father, making marriage the only feasible alternative. Perhaps she reckons, as well, that her money-careless father cannot afford to support her forever and therefore that she should marry to lighten the debts that have become his constant companion.

The object of her affections is Joseph Alston, the son of a wealthy South Carolina planter. Alston seems not to be intimidated by Theo, as many potential suitors are. He enjoys matching wits with her, and she delights in testing him. "My father laughs at my impatience to hear from you, and says I am in love," she writes him. "But I do not believe that to be a fair deduction, for the post is really very irregular and slow—enough so to provoke anybody." Alston is impatient, too, and presses her to marry him, though she is only seventeen and he twenty-one. She replies matter-of-factly: "I had not intended to marry this twelvemonth." But she allows him to make his case. "Aristotle says that 'a man should not marry before he is six-and-thirty.' Pray, Mr. Alston, what arguments have you to oppose to such authority?"

"Hear me, Miss Burr," he responds. "It has always been my practice, whether from a natural independence of mind, from pride, or what other cause I will not pretend to say, never to adopt the opinion of any one, however respectable his authority, unless thoroughly convinced by his arguments. The 'ipse dixit,' as logicians term it, even of Cicero, who stands higher in my estimation than any other author, would not have the least weight with me. You must therefore, till you offer better reasons in support of his opinion than the Grecian sage himself has done, excuse my differing from him." The sound objections to early marriage arise solely from want of fortune or want of discretion, Alston says. Fortune is no issue in the present case, he observes. As for discretion: "The age of discretion is wholly uncertain, some men reaching it at twenty, others at thirty, some again not till fifty, and many not at all. . . . To fix such or such a period as the proper one for marrying is ridiculous." But even allowing a general rule to exist, are there not exceptions? "Suppose (*for instance, merely*) a young man nearly two-and-twenty, already of the *greatest* discretion, with an ample fortune, were to be passionately in love with a young lady almost eighteen, equally discreet with himself, and who had a 'sincere friendship' for him—do you think it would be necessary to make him wait till thirty, particularly where the friends on both sides were pleased with the match?"

Moving from the (barely) hypothetical to the demonstrable, Alston sketches his upbringing, as it bears on the question at hand. In certain respects it has mirrored hers. "From my father's plan of education for me, I may properly be called a hot-bed plant. Introduced from my infancy into the society of men, while yet a boy I was accustomed to think and act like a man. On every occasion, however important, I was left to decide for myself; I do not recollect a single instance where I was controlled even by advice; for it was my father's invariable maxim, that the best way of strengthening the judgment was to suffer it to be constantly exercised. Before seventeen I finished my college education; before twenty I was admitted to the bar. Since that time I have been constantly travelling through different parts of the United States; to what purpose I leave you to determine."

The prejudice against marrying young is indeed a prejudice, Alston explains, and in fact is the opposite of wisdom. Theo has cited Aristotle; Alston adduces a source closer to their own era and country. "Dr. Franklin, a very strong advocate for my system, and, I think, at least as good authority as Aristotle, very aptly compares those who marry early to two young trees joined together by the hand of the gardener:

Trunk knit with trunk, and branch with branch intwined,
Advancing still, more closely they are join'd;
At length, full grown, no difference we see,
But, 'stead of two, behold a single tree!

9

Impressed by his logic as well as his passion, Theo accepts Alston's arguments, and the couple are wed at the beginning of 1801. Burr blesses the union and lays plans to visit his daughter at her new South Carolina home. "I am to be detained here yet a week," he writes Theo from Washington shortly after being sworn in as vice president. "On my return to New York I shall prepare for a tour to Georgetown or Charleston, probably a water passage." He has taken to confiding his amours to Theo, who appreciates his humor when he promises: "Nothing but *matrimony* will prevent my voyage to Charleston and Georgetown; and even so great an event shall only postpone, but not defeat, the project. I am sorry, however, to add that I have no expectations or decided views on this subject. I mean Hymen."

Other gods, however—of the storm—conspire against him. "On Wednesday, the 18th, I left the great city," he writes in late March. "At the Susquehanna the wind was rude; the river, swollen by recent rains, was rapid. The ferrymen pronounced it to be impossible to pass with horses, and unsafe to attempt it. By the logic of money and brandy I persuaded them to attempt it. We embarked; the wind was, indeed, too mighty for us, and we drove on the rocks; but the boat did not bilge or fill, as in all reason it ought to have done. I left Alexis and Harry"—two traveling companions—"to work out their way; got my precious carcass transported in a skiff, and went on in a stage to pass a day with 'thee and thou'"—the Quakers of Pennsylvania. He finds their calm, quiet outlook impressive. "How charming, how enviable is this equanimity, if real. There is one invaluable attainment in the education of this sect, one which you and I never thought of: it is *tacere*"—to be silent. He teases her: "How particularly desirable this in a wife."

He arrives at New York, but, in the absence of his darling, the city holds little cheer. "I approached home as I would approach the sepulchre of all my friends. Dreary, solitary, comfortless. It was no longer *home*." He counts the days till he can see her. "I am preparing with all imaginable zeal for a voyage to Charleston. . . . I hope to be at sea by the 20th of April. . . . In eight days you shall know more of this."

On April 15 he writes that he hopes to embark momentarily. "The ship *South Carolina* is now in port, and will sail on Monday next. I wish to take passage in her." But complications arise. "A thousand concerns of business and obstacles of various kinds appear to oppose. I shall combat them all with the zeal which my ardent wishes for the voyage inspire; yet I dare hardly hope to succeed. You shall hear again by the mail of Saturday."

The *South Carolina* sails without him. Politics, in particular the rivalry between his Republicans and Hamilton's Federalists, keeps him in New York. "Our election commences to-morrow, and will be open for three days," he tells Theo. "The Republican members of the assembly for this city"—the city's delegation to the lower house in Albany—"will be carried by a greater majority than last year, unless some fraud be practised at the polls. The corporation"—the municipal government—"have had the indecent hardiness to appoint known and warm Federalists (and no others) to be inspectors of the election in every ward. Hamilton works day and night with the most intemperate and outrageous zeal, but I think wholly without effect."

Two days later he confesses defeat—not in politics, where he has triumphed, but in his plans to see her. "This morning will sail the brig *Echo*, the only vessel in harbor destined for South Carolina. I do not go in her. With unspeakable regret, therefore, the projected visit is abandoned—wholly and absolutely abandoned." He knows she will be disappointed, but not as much as he is. "The pain of my own disappointment leaves me no room for any sympathy with yours."

He fills her in, a little, on the other affairs of his heart. "I had like to have forgotten to say a word in reply to your inquiries of matrimony, which would seem to indicate that I have no plan on the subject. Such is the fact. You are or were my projector in this line. If perchance I should have one, it will be executed before you will hear of the design. Yet I ought not to conceal that I have had a most amiable overture from a lady 'who is always employed in something useful'"—an ironic phrase he and Theo share in humor. "She was, you know, a few months past, engaged to another; that other is suspended, if not quite dismissed. If I should meet her, and she should challenge me, I should probably strike at once."

He comforts himself that though he cannot travel south to see her, she might come north to visit him. She arranges to do so, and he eagerly marks his calendar. "You must not delay your voyage hither," he says at subsequently hearing of a hitch in the plans. He misses her voice and her face—and her wisdom. "I want your counsel and your exertions in an important negotiation, actually commenced, but not advancing, and which will probably be stationary until your arrival; more probably it may, however, in the mean time, retrograde." She knows he is speaking of a love affair; he will identify the lady when they meet.

He shows Theo off when she and Alston arrive. His friends and acquaintances grow more admiring than ever. "You made two, perhaps more, conquests on your Northern tour—King Brant and the stage driver; both of whom have been profuse in their eulogies," he writes after the visit. King Brant is the Mohawk chief. "Brant has written me two letters on the subject. It would have been quite in style if he had scalped your husband and made you Queen of the Mohawks."

The conversations they conduct in person while she is in New York are continued by mail after she leaves. "You women: it is so with you all," he writes. "If one wishes to exhibit the best side, one must provoke you. Gratify your wishes and expectations, or, still worse, anticipate them, and it produces a lethargy." He speaks more specifically: "How have I laboured for three months, working and writing to please a certain lady: nothing comes but inanity and torpor. I provoke her, and behold the effusions of spirit and genius. Be assured that I shall not speedily relapse into the same error. Indeed, I knew all this before. But I thought it was only one's mistress that was to be thus managed; it is the sex." He facetiously blames her for the sins of womanhood—and for his rambling on. "This is dull. I had something more cheerful to say; this, however, came first, and would have place. And here am I, at midnight, talking such stuff to bagatelle, and twenty unanswered letters of *vast importance* before me! Get to bed, you hussy."

IO

"*You have learned from the newspapers (which you never* read) the death of Philip Hamilton," he writes her in late 1801. "Shot in a duel with Eacker, the lawyer. Some dispute at a theatre, arising, as is said, out of politics."

Philip Hamilton was the son of Alexander Hamilton, and his death reveals the emotions aroused by politics as the party system takes hold in the young republic. The traditional forms of deference are giving way to the new dynamics of democracy, but the transition is difficult and at times deadly. Several states, including New York, have outlawed dueling, but the practice persists among those who consider themselves men of honor. Sometimes they fight one another, sometimes they respond to outsiders who deem dueling an entrée to their ranks. The duelists' friends and families are ambivalent: neither sufficiently supportive to maintain the practice in its old form nor sufficiently shocked to prevent the issue and acceptance of challenges.

Burr pays little attention. He engages in political disputes but tries to keep them in perspective. He also tries to keep busy. His responsibilities as vice president are few, consisting primarily of presiding over the Senate. He wields the gavel with skill and aplomb. But he is rarely consulted by Jefferson, who hopes to groom friend and fellow Virginian Madison for the succession to the presidency. Hamilton hates Burr as much as ever and poisons the minds of all who will listen, limiting Burr's present prospects further.

More interesting to Burr than the vice presidency is the news that he will be a grandfather. Suddenly Theo is his child again, needing paternal advice. "You must walk a great deal," he writes her. "It is the only exercise you can take with safety and advantage, and, being in Charleston, I fear you will neglect it. I do entreat you to get a very stout pair of over shoes, or short boots, to draw on over your shoes. But shoes to come up to the ankle bone, with one button to keep them on, will be best." Alston will not always be able to walk with her. "You must learn to walk without your husband—alone—or, if you must be in form, with ten negroes at your heels."

The child, a boy, arrives safely. Theo names him after her father, and Aaron Burr Alston becomes his grandfather's favorite male person. She avoids the South Carolina summer by traveling north once more, this time bringing little Aaron with her. She revels in the familiar settings. "Never did I behold this island so beautiful," she writes her husband from Manhattan. "The variety of vivid greens; the finely-cultivated fields and gaudy gardens; the neat, cool air of the city's boxes, peeping through straight rows of tall poplars, and the elegance of some gentlemen's seats, commanding a view of the majestic Hudson, and the high, dark shores of New Jersey, altogether form a scene so lively, so touching, and to me now so new, that I was in constant rapture."

A traveling companion's fascination with New York highlights her own sense of the virtues of her native environs. "S. appears more pleased with New York than any person I ever saw from South Carolina," she writes Alston. "With the beauty of the country it is impossible not to be delighted, whether that delight is confessed or not; and every woman cannot fail to prefer the style of society, whatever she may say. If she denies it, she is set down in my mind as insincere and weakly prejudiced."

She proves herself her father's daughter when she admonishes Alston to watch his health. "Before my departure you complained grievously of the bad cigars sold in Charleston. In the hope that this city affords better, I send you a box containing a thousand; the seller took some trouble to choose the best for me, and I have added some Vanilla and Tonka beans to them. May the offering please my great Apollo!" The cigars are for health as much as for pleasure. "If you should do so rash a thing as to visit the city during the summer, pray smoke all the time you remain there; it creates an atmosphere round you, and prevents impure air from reaching you." Any city visits should take place in the afternoon or evening. "I have somewhere heard that persons were less apt to catch infectious disorders at that time than any other, and I believe it." She explains her reasoning: "Have you never remarked how highly scented the air is before sunrise in a flower garden, so much so as to render the smell of any flower totally imperceptible if you put it to your nose? That is, I suppose, because, when the sun acts with all his force, the air becomes so rarefied, that the quantity of perfume you inhale at a breath can have no effect; while, on the contrary, during the night, the vapours become so condensed that you perceive them in every blast. May not the same be the case with noxious vapours?" She admits that this is only a theory. "Perhaps I am wrong both in my reason and opinion. If so, you are able to correct; only do as you think best, and be prudent. It is all I ask. I imagine the subject worth a reflection, and you cannot err. Montesquieu says he writes to make people think; and why may not Theodosia?"

She misses her husband and charms his thoughts with an imagined improvement on correspondence. "What a pity minds could not be made sensible of each other's approach! Why were we not so formed, that when your thoughts, your soul were with your Theo, hers could be enabled, by the finest sensation of sympathy, to meet it? How superior to writing would that be! A letter is a month old before it is received; by that time other thoughts and subjects engage the writer. The sentiments expressed in it seem no longer warm from the heart. I have been all this evening divining your occupation. Sometimes I imagine you writing or reading, and then the hope that you are thinking of me arises. Pray what have you been doing? If you can possibly recollect, let me know."

Amid her pleasure in her father's company and the

reminders of her childhood, she contracts a summer fever. Her father shares his concern with her husband. "The debility and loss of appetite which your wife has experienced alarmed me," Burr writes Alston. The physicians recommend that she wean her baby or engage a wet nurse. "This she peremptorily refused, and the bare proposition occasioned so many tears and so much distress that I abandoned it. Within the last three days, however, she has such a loss of appetite and prostration of strength, that she is satisfied of the necessity of the measure for the sake of the child, if not for herself; and I have this day sent off a man to the country to find a suitable nurse."

Theo's physical troubles linger. She has not entirely recuperated from young Aaron's delivery; internal bleeding and a stubborn infection cause her discomfort and occasional disability. She grows discouraged, judging her malady chronic. "I have now abandoned all hope of recovery," she writes Alston. "I do not say it in a moment of depression, but with all my reason about me. I am endeavouring to resign myself with cheerfulness; and you also, my husband, must summon up your fortitude to bear with a sick wife the rest of her life. At present, my general health is very good; indeed, my appearance so perfectly announces it, that physicians smile at the idea of my being an invalid. The great misfortune of this complaint is, that one may vegetate forty years in a sort of middle state between life and death, without the enjoyment of one or the rest of the other."

Burr believes she exaggerates. "The cold weather of the

last ten days has had a happy effect on Theodosia," he writes Alston in November 1802, as she is preparing to sail for home. "She is so far restored that I can with confidence assure you she will return in health." Nor is she alone in thriving on the cold. "The boy, too, grows fat and rosy with the frost." Burr tells Alston that the voyage will be comfortable. "She will have the control of the cabin, and will be perfectly well accommodated." He hates to see her go but won't hinder her departure. "I regret she will sail so soon (the 12th), as well because I cannot attend her as that I could have wished her health and that of the boy to have been still more confirmed. Yet I cannot any longer resist her impatience. . . . When you shall see her and son, you will not regret this five months' separation."

He distrusts ocean travel and worries till word comes that she has reached home safely. "I drank a bottle of champagne on the occasion," he writes her. Yet he scolds her that he first got the news from another source. "Though this relieves me from the great anxiety under which I laboured, still there are many details of your passage, your arrival, &c., on which nothing but your letter can satisfy me. . . . Had it not been for the intelligence by water of your safe arrival, we should have concluded that you and Kate"—a cousin traveling with her—"were now dancing with Amphitrite. How jealous her majesty would have been at the presence of two such rivals."

———

He is distressed to hear that she has suffered a relapse in South Carolina, but he is encouraged by the pluck she displays. "I was one night so ill as to have lost my senses," she writes. "About daylight, as a last resource, they began plying me with old wine, and blisters to my feet. But, on recovering a little, I kicked off the blisters, and declared I would be dressed; be carried in the open air, and have free use of cold water. I was indulged. I was carried below, where I drank plentifully of cold water, and I had my face, neck, and arms bathed with it, and it assisted most astonishingly in recovering me. The day before yesterday I was put on a bed in a boat and brought here." She is writing from Clifton in the South Carolina upcountry. "The change of air and scene have assisted me wonderfully. I am again getting well. Indeed, the rapidity with which I gain strength surprises the whole family."

Her secret, she says, is to treat her illness as a man would. "I exert myself to the utmost, feeling none of that pride, so common to my sex, of being weak and ill. Delicacy and debility are sometimes fascinating when affected by a coquette, adorned with the freshness of health; but a pale, thin face; sunken, instead of languishing eyes; and a form, evidently tottering, not gracefully bending, never, I suspect, made, far less could they retain a conquest, or even please a friend. I therefore encourage spirits, try to appear well, and am rewarded. In a few days I shall be on the high road to health."

But she can't yet be as active as she wishes, and she relates to her father her impatience at being idle. "The longer I live, the more frequently the truth of your advice evinces itself, and never was there anything more true than that occupation is necessary to give one command over themselves. I confess I feel myself growing quite cross on the journey, and it is really to be feared that, unless we soon finish it, the serene tranquility of my placid temper may be injured." She spurns the romance novels favored for entertainment by other women. "Novel reading has, I find, not only the ill effect of rendering people romantic, which, thanks to my father on earth, I am long past, but they really furnish no occupation to the mind. A series of events follow so rapidly, and are interwoven with remarks so commonplace and so spun out, that there is nothing left to reflect upon. A collection of images, which amuse only from their variety and rapid succession, like the pictures of a magic lantern—not like a piece of Vanderlyn, where the painter makes fine touches, and leaves to your vanity at least the merit of discovering them."

Father and daughter exchange views on matters small and large. He consults her on a plan for swapping Rich-

mond Hill for a rural Manhattan estate that once belonged
to merchant and financier Roger Morris. Richmond Hill
isn't the same without her, he says, and the Morris place
appears a bargain. She weighs the proposition. "Richmond
Hill will, for a few years to come, be more valuable than
Morris's," she observes. "And to you, who are so fond of
town, a place so far from it would be useless. So much for
my reasoning on one side; now for the other. Richmond
Hill has lost many of its beauties, and is daily losing more."
The city is encroaching on all sides. "If you mean it for a
residence, what avail its intrinsic value? If you sell part,
you deprive it of every beauty save the mere view. Morris's
is the most commanding view on the island. It is reputed
to be indescribably beautiful. The grounds are pretty. How
many delightful walks can be made on one hundred and
thirty acres! How much of your taste displayed! In ten or
twenty years hence, one hundred and thirty acres on New
York island will be a principality; and there is to me something stylish, elegant, respectable and suitable to you in
having a handsome country seat. So that, upon the whole,
I vote for Morris's."

Burr weighs the advice; meanwhile Theo hears a rumor
that he has been wounded in a duel with Andrew Jackson.
He responds by return mail: "This is only to assure you
that I am in perfect health. That General Jackson is my
good friend; that I have had no duel nor quarrel with anybody, and have not been wounded or hurt."

He relates his most recent love affairs. "La G. may be
forty-one," he says of a current flame. "Something of the

style and manners of *la tante de La R.*"—another lover, whom Theo knows. "Is about as silly; talks as much, and as much nonsense; is certainly good-tempered and cheerful; rather comely, abating a flat chest; about two inches taller than Theodosia. Things are not gone to extremities; but there is danger."

He sends instructions for her next visit. "Bring no horse nor carriage. I have got a nice, new, beautiful little chariot, made purposely to please you. I have also a new coachee, very light, on an entire new construction. . . . These two machines are severally adapted to two horses, and you may take your choice of them." Nor need she bring servants. "Of servants there are enough for family purposes." She, Alston and young Aaron shall have Richmond Hill to themselves. "I shall take rooms (a house, &c.) in town, but will live with you as much or as little as you may please and as we can agree."

He gently scolds her for not writing more about his grandson. "You have been remarkably reserved in your two last letters. I conclude, however, that he cannot be dead, as you would, probably, have thought that a circumstance worthy of being mentioned, at least in a postscript." When she appends the boy's first scribbles, he is thrilled. "I have studied every pothook and trammel of his first literary performance, to see what rays of genius could be discovered," he says. "You remember our friend Schweitzer, nephew and pupil of Lavater. He used to insist that as much was to be inferred from the handwriting as from the face. I showed him a letter from a man of great fame, and he saw genius in every stroke. I then produced a letter from an arrant blockhead and great knave, but so like the other as not to be distinguished, at least by my unphysiognomical discernment. He acknowledged that there was resemblance to an ignorant eye; but, said he, triumphantly, this (latter) could never have made that scratch, which sybilistic scratch was the mere prolongation of the last letter of the last word in a sentence. Now it occurs to me that one of A.B.A.'s scratches is exactly in the line of genius according to Schweitzer; and surely more may be presumed from the instinctive effort of untutored infancy than from the laboured essay of scientific cultivation."

12

Burr's joy is *Theo* and *Aaron; his job is politics. And his*
political fortunes are declining, from causes he cannot
control. Jefferson once assailed political parties as inimical
to the public interest, but the Virginian has proved himself an adept, even ruthless, party leader. He exploited
Burr's deftness in delivering New York in the 1800 election, but now he prefers Madison, a man more after his
own tastes and over whom he expects to wield more influence. Though relations between Jefferson and Burr remain
personally polite, the president employs patronage and
other perquisites of office to advance Madison's prospects
and retard Burr's. The opposition Federalists, who are
slouching toward inconsequence, can't decide whether to
cultivate Burr or excoriate him. Most adopt the latter
course, which might have endeared Burr to Jefferson had
the president not already chosen another protégé; the
result is simply to impugn Burr's integrity and cloud his
political future.

The maneuvers occur in a social welter that often cannot locate the boundary between the personal and the

political. Elected officials and candidates are slandered and libeled in the most scurrilous manner, their personal beliefs, habits and relationships recounted in terms that show no respect for honor and precious little for truth. George Washington retired after two terms as president not least because he couldn't stand the lies attached to his name by hostile journalists. John Adams wanted a second term but didn't miss the insults and innuendos he had endured. Jefferson hears that he is a Satanist, the Antichrist and any number of other outlandish allegations, and he doubtless does *not* hear the most egregious of the slanders, which circulate beyond the realm of the published word.

Burr too is the target of venom. In the late winter of 1804 he arranges for friends in the New York legislature to nominate him for governor. Election, should he win, will afford a most respectable exit from the Jefferson administration and provide a base for a subsequent attempt at the presidency. The nomination at once arouses Alexander Hamilton to mount a campaign against him. "Hamilton is intriguing for any candidate who can have a chance of success against A. B.," Burr writes Theo. Hamilton and Burr's other opponents circulate criticism of him, alleging everything from political intrigue to moral turpitude. Broadsides and handbills assert that he has seduced innocent young women, who have borne his bastard children in the brothels to which they have been confined since he ruined them. He writes Theo about "the new and amusing libels" regularly perpetrated against him, but he publicly declines to take notice.

As election day approaches, the furor intensifies. Theo's most recent letter has been composed in a thunderstorm; he answers: "I, too, write in a storm: an election storm, of the like you have once been a witness. The thing began yesterday, and will terminate tomorrow. . . . Both parties claim majorities, and there never was, in my opinion, an election of the result of which so little judgment could be formed. A. B. will have a small majority in this city—if tomorrow should be a fair day."

He does win in New York City, but he loses the state as a whole. He takes the result philosophically. "The election is lost by a great majority," he writes Theo. *"Tant mieux"*— so much the better. The decisiveness of the defeat makes clear that his future, for some while at least, will not be in politics. He can return to the practice of law, recoup his fortunes and prepare for whatever might ensue. Not least, he will have more time for Theo and young Aaron.

But one loose end needs tying off. During the campaign a letter written by a Dr. Cooper had been reprinted in the Federalist press. "General Hamilton and Judge Kent have declared in substance that they looked upon Mr. Burr to be a dangerous man, and one who ought not to be trusted with the reins of government," the Cooper letter avers. It continues: "I could detail to you a still more despicable opinion which General Hamilton has expressed of Mr. Burr."

Burr didn't read the letter when it was published, and he encounters it only when it is shown to him after the election. He decides that Hamilton's assaults have gone far enough. He drafts a note to his adversary. "You must perceive, sir, the necessity of a prompt and unqualified acknowledgment or denial of the use of any expression which would warrant the assertions of Dr. Cooper," he says. He hands the note to a friend who delivers it to Hamilton.

Hamilton hadn't seen the Cooper letter either. He asks for time to respond. And when he does respond, he neither acknowledges nor denies the language attributed to him. "Between gentlemen, *despicable* and *more despicable* are not worth the pains of distinction," he says. He rejects the premise of Burr's note. "I deem it inadmissible on principle to consent to be interrogated as to the justness of the inferences which may be drawn by others from whatever I may have said of a political opponent in the course of fifteen years competition."

Burr interprets Hamilton's response as smug equivocation. "I regret to find in it nothing of that sincerity and delicacy which you profess to value," he says. "Political opposition can never absolve gentlemen from the necessity of a rigid adherence to the laws of honor and the rules of decorum. I neither claim such privilege nor indulge it in others. . . . Your letter has furnished me with new reasons for requiring a definite reply."

Hamilton's neck stiffens, too. "If by a 'definite reply' you mean the direct avowal or disavowal required in your first letter," he says, "I have no other answer to give than that which has already been given."

Intermediaries attempt to arrest the escalating tension. Several days are filled with their efforts to find language that will suit the honor of both parties. Should either side evince a desire to de-escalate, the mediation must succeed. And should either Hamilton or Burr not feel his political future in jeopardy, that party must surely yield to common sense. But Hamilton has alienated many of the Federalists, and the party as a whole is falling apart; he has no margin for magnanimity. Burr has been cast aside by Jefferson and hence the Republican majority; he, too, cannot risk being seen as weak. So each man holds his ground, more stubbornly with every message that passes between them.

Burr, finally concluding that Hamilton will never own or disclaim the assertions attributed to him, directs the delivery of a challenge. "Colonel Burr disavows all motives of predetermined hostility," the message says. "He feels as a gentleman should feel when his honor is impeached or assailed; and, without sensations of hostility or wishes of revenge, he is determined to vindicate that honor at such hazard as the nature of the case demands."

13

He has declined to inform Theo of the conflict as it develops. "Yesterday we kept Theo's birthday," he writes on June 24, as the notes are flying back and forth. "The Laights and half a dozen others laughed an hour, and danced an hour, and drank her health at Richmond Hill. We had your picture in the dining room; but, as it is a profile, and would not look at us, we hung it up and placed Natalie's at table, which laughs and talks with us." Theo recently suggested a writing scheme. "Your idea of dressing up pieces of ancient mythology in the form of amusing tales for children is very good," he responds. "You yourself must write them. Send your performances to me, and, within three weeks after they are received, you shall have them again in print. This will be not only an amusing occupation, but a very useful one to yourself. It will improve your style and your language, give you habits of accuracy, and add a little to your stock of knowledge." He merely hints of the troubles at hand. "You laugh at me so much and so impudently, that I will not say a word more of certain things till something be concluded. Your permission seems to be that I may hang or drown, or make any other apotheosis I may please. Dear indulgent creature, how I thank thee."

A week later, as the crisis approaches, he conveys another hint. "Having been shivering with cold all day, though in perfect health, I have now, just at sunset, had a fire in my library, and am sitting near it and enjoying it, if that word be applicable to anything done in solitude. Some very wise man, however, has exclaimed,

Oh! fools, who think it solitude to be alone.

This is but poetry. Let us, therefore, drop the subject, lest it lead to another on which I have imposed silence on myself."

But finally he reveals what is afoot. "I have called out General Hamilton, and we meet tomorrow morning," he writes Alston on July 10. "If it should be my lot to fall, yet I shall live in you and your son. I commit to you all that is most dear to me—my reputation and my daughter. Your talents and your attachment will be the guardian of the one, your kindness and your generosity of the other." He asks his son-in-law to encourage his wife and child in their intellectual endeavors. "Let me entreat you to stimulate and aid Theodosia in the cultivation of her mind. It is indispensable to her happiness and essential to yours. It is also of the utmost importance to your son. She would presently acquire a critical knowledge of Latin, English, and all branches of natural philosophy. All this would be poured into your son. If you should differ with me as to the importance of this measure, suffer me to ask it of you as a last favor. She will richly compensate your trouble."

He saves his last words for Theo. "Having lately written my will, and given my private letters and papers in charge to you," he writes, "I have no other direction to give you on the subject but to request you to burn all such as, if by accident made public, would injure any person. This is more particularly applicable to the letters of my female correspondents." One batch is especially sensitive. "Burn immediately a small bundle, tied with a red string, which you will find in the little flat writing-case—that which we used with the curricle." Other materials should be saved. "All my letters, and copies of letters, of which I have retained copies, are in the six blue boxes. If your husband or anyone else (no one, however, could do it so well as he) should think it worthwhile to write a sketch of my life, some materials will be found among these letters."

He asks her to dispose of his property. "My estate will just about pay my debts and no more—I mean, if I should die this year. If I live a few years, it is probable things may be better." She should look after his few household slaves. He has granted freedom to Peggy and has conveyed to her a small parcel of land. "Give her also fifty dollars in cash as a reward for her fidelity." A second slave woman, Nancy—"honest, robust, and good-tempered"—should be retained, sold or emancipated as Theo sees fit. A young male slave, Peter, will make a fine servant for Aaron. "Peter is the most intelligent and best-disposed black I have ever known. . . . I advise you, by all means, to keep him as the valet of your son."

His parting sentiment offers his gratitude and benediction. "I am indebted to you, my dearest Theodosia, for a very great portion of the happiness which I have enjoyed in this life. You have completely satisfied all that my heart and affections had hoped or even wished. With a little more perseverance, determination, and industry, you will obtain all that my ambition or vanity had fondly imagined. Let your son have occasion to be proud that he had a mother. Adieu. Adieu."

14

He lies down on the couch in his library and sleeps till dawn.
A friend finds him slumbering and rouses him. Two other
friends arrive, and the group walks down to the Hudson
bank, where a boat waits. Oarsmen row them across to
Weehawken, New Jersey, to a sheltered ledge that frequently serves as a dueling ground. New Jersey's legislature
has, like New York's, outlawed dueling, but prosecutions
are less certain than in New York. The seconds have
arranged for Hamilton to arrive a half-hour later, lest two
boats together stir the suspicions of the man who owns the
property and vigorously opposes dueling. Whenever he
learns of an imminent duel, he races from his house and
throws himself between the duelists, refusing to leave until
they consent not to shoot each other.

Burr and Hamilton exchange terse greetings. Their
seconds establish the dueling distance—ten paces—and
determine by lot the choice of position. Hamilton's man
wins the choice, and for reasons best known to himself has
Hamilton face east, into the rising sun.

The pistols are loaded. The principals take their marks.

Hamilton's second explains that he will ask if they are ready; on their affirmative he will say, "Present." They may then fire as soon as they wish. Burr and Hamilton nod.

Hamilton's second looks to each. "Are you ready?" he asks. They nod again.

"Present," he says.

Burr at once aims and fires. His ball hits Hamilton, who fires convulsively as he falls, his shot going astray. Burr steps toward the slumping Hamilton, ready to offer assistance. But his second, fearing that the gunshots will attract inquisitive persons who might serve as witnesses in the event of a prosecution, grasps his arm and leads him back to the boat. The oarsmen propel them swiftly to Richmond Hill, where he goes into seclusion.

A doctor tends to Hamilton, who lives, but barely. The wounded man is carried to his boat and likewise transported across the river. He is taken to the home of a friend, ironically near Richmond Hill, and placed on a bed. He drifts in and out of consciousness the rest of that day and through the night. He receives his wife and seven children, who haven't known of the duel until they learn that the head of their family has been gravely shot. He weakens with the new day but clings to life till early afternoon, when he finally expires.

15

"*General Hamilton died yesterday,*" Burr informs Alston. "The malignant Federalists or Tories, and the embittered Clintonians"—supporters of longtime New York governor George Clinton—"unite in endeavouring to excite public sympathy in his favour and indignation against his antagonist. Thousands of absurd falsehoods are circulated with industry. The most illiberal means are practised in order to produce excitement, and, for the moment, with effect."

He is genuinely surprised. Affairs of honor are supposed to be personal matters, but his enemies are exploiting this one for political effect. He hopes the hubbub will diminish, given time. "I propose leaving town for a few days, and meditate also a journey for some weeks," he tells Alston. "But whither is not resolved. . . . You will hear from me again in about eight days."

He travels to Philadelphia, where a friend takes him in. The hundred miles that now separate him from the scene of the duel provide a necessary cushion. "Our most unprincipled Jacobins"—the extreme Jeffersonians—"are the loudest in their lamentations for the death of General

Hamilton, whom, for many years, they have uniformly represented as the most detestable and unprincipled of men," Burr writes Alston. "The motives are obvious. Every sort of persecution is to be exercised against me. A coroner's jury will sit this evening, being the fourth time. The object of this unexampled measure is to obtain an inquest of murder. Upon this a warrant will issue to apprehend me, and, if I should be taken, no bail would probably be allowed. You know enough of the temper and principles of the generality of the officers of our state government to form a judgment of my position."

He writes more reassuringly to Theo. "You will have learned, through Mr. Alston, of certain measures pursuing against me in New York. I absent myself from home merely to give a little time for passions to subside, not from any apprehension of the final effects of proceedings in courts of law. They can, by no possibility, eventually affect my person. You will find the papers filled with all manner of nonsense and lies. Among other things, accounts of attempts to assassinate me. These, I assure you, are mere fables. Those who wish me dead prefer to keep at a very respectful distance. No such attempt has been made nor will be made. I walk and ride about here as usual."

All the same, he concludes that a journey farther south is prudent. A friend, Pierce Butler, gives refuge at a plantation on the Georgia coast. "I am now quite settled," he writes Theo from St. Simon's in late August. "My establishment consists of a housekeeper, cook, and chambermaid, seamstress, and two footmen. There are, besides, two fishermen and four bargemen always at command. The department of laundress is done abroad. The plantation affords plenty of milk, cream, and butter; turkeys, fowls, kids, pigs, geese, and mutton; fish, of course, in abundance. Of figs, peaches, and melons there are yet a few. Oranges and pomegranates just begin to be eatable. The house affords Madeira wine, brandy, and porter." The locals are as friendly as can be. "Yesterday my neighbour, Mr. Couper, sent me an assortment of French wines, consisting of Claret, Sauterne, and Champagne, all excellent; and at least a twelve months' supply of orange shrub, which makes a most delicious punch. Madame Couper added sweetmeats and pickles." He has rarely enjoyed such a holiday; he writes Theo that he has landed almost in paradise. "We have not a fly, moscheto, or bug. I can sit a whole evening, with open windows and lighted candles, without the least annoyance from insects; a circumstance which I have never beheld in any other place. I have not even seen a cockroach."

He arrived in the lee of a hurricane. "The cotton in this neighbourhood, on the coast southward to the extremity of Florida, and northward as far as we have heard, has been totally destroyed. The crop of Mr. C. was supposed to be worth one hundred thousand dollars, and not an extravagant estimate, for he has eight hundred slaves. He will not get enough to pay half the expenses of the plantation. Yet he laughs about it with good humour and without affectation. Butler suffers about half this loss. Part of his force had been turned to rice."

Two weeks later a second hurricane slams the island. Burr has heard that Couper is ill, and he goes to visit him. "When about to return in the evening, the wind had risen so that, after an ineffectual attempt, I was obliged to give it up, and remain at Mr. C.'s," he writes Theo. "In the morning the wind was still higher. It continued to rise, and by noon blew a gale from the north, which, together with the swelling of the water, became alarming. From twelve to three, several of the out-houses had been destroyed; most of the trees about the house were blown down. The house in which we were shook and rocked so much that Mr. C. began to express his apprehensions for our safety. Before three, part of the piazza was carried away; two or three of the windows bursted in. The house was inundated with water, and presently one of the chimneys fell. Mr. C. then commanded a retreat to a storehouse about fifty yards off, and we decamped, men, women, and children. You may imagine, in this scene of confusion and dismay, a good many incidents to amuse one if one had dared to be amused in a moment of much anxiety. The house, however, did not blow down. The storm continued till four, and then very suddenly abated, and in ten minutes it was almost a calm. I seized the moment to return home."

But this was merely the eye of the hurricane. "Before I had got quite over, the gale rose from the southeast and threatened new destruction. It lasted a great part of the night, but did not attain the violence of that from the north; yet it contributed to raise still higher the water, which was the principal instrument of devastation. The flood was about seven feet above the height of an ordinary high tide. This has been sufficient to inundate a great part of the coast; to destroy all the rice; to carry off most of the buildings which were on low lands, and to destroy the lives of many blacks. The roads are rendered impassable, and scarcely a boat has been preserved. . . . Major Butler has lost nineteen negroes (drowned), and I fear his whole crop of rice, being about two hundred and sixty acres. Mr. Brailsford, of Charleston, who cultivates in rice an island at the mouth of the Alatamaha, has lost, reports say, seventy-four blacks."

Burr hoped to travel still farther south, but the storms change his plans. "To get to Florida seems now impracticable; nor do any present means occur of getting from this island in any direction." Neither is it likely the mail will get through. Burr closes his letter to Theo by explaining the trials its carrier will have to overcome. "This letter goes to Savannah by a negro who has to swim half a dozen creeks, in one of which, at least, it is probable he may drown." She will hear from him when conditions improve.

16

He is back in Washington by early November. While he presides over the Senate he is immune from prosecution, but the wheels of justice grind forward, anticipating the end of the session. He tries to maintain a sense of humor about his predicament. "You have doubtless heard that there has subsisted for some time a contention of a very singular nature between the states of New York and New Jersey," he writes Theo. "To what lengths it may go, or how it may terminate, cannot be predicted; but, as you will take some interest in the question, I will state it for your satisfaction and consideration. The subject in dispute is which shall have the honour of hanging the vice-president." He says he personally hasn't developed a preference between the two. But he assures her she won't be kept in the dark. "You shall have due notice of the time and place. Whenever it may be, you may rely on a great concourse of company, much gayety, and many rare sights; such as the lion, the elephant, &c."

It doesn't come to that. Jefferson's thrashing of Federalist Charles Pinckney in the 1804 election—the tally among the electors, conducted under the provisions of the newly adopted Twelfth Amendment, is 162 for Jefferson and running mate George Clinton to 14 for Pinckney and Rufus King—reminds the Federalists they have greater problems than Burr. The Republicans have no desire to revive Hamilton. The prosecutions are quietly suspended.

Burr completes his service as vice president with a grace that moves his friends and silences his enemies. He sits as judge in the impeachment trial of Supreme Court justice Samuel Chase, which pits Jefferson's Republican allies against Chase and the Federalists. Chase's outspoken opposition to the president and his party has annoyed the Republicans, who have arranged the impeachment as a way of slapping him down. Yet Chase is acquitted, under Burr's oversight, and the verdict leaves Jefferson frustrated with the Federalists and angry at Burr for failing to remember his Republican roots. "He conducted the trial with the dignity and impartiality of an angel, but with the rigor of a devil," an observer notes.

Burr takes his leave of the Senate in a speech that reminds members of his rhetorical gifts. "I am sensible that I must at times have wounded the feelings of individual members," he says. "I avoided entering into explanations at the time, because a moment of irritation is not a moment for explanation." For his part, he has no injuries to complain of. "If any have been done or attempted, I am ignorant of the authors. If I have ever heard, I have forgotten, for, thank God, I have no memory for injuries." Where he misstepped, he did so from worthy motives.

"My errors, whatever they may have been, were those of rule and principle, and not of caprice. . . . If, in the opinion of any, the discipline which has been established approached to rigor, you will at least admit that it was uniform and indiscriminate."

Members might differ on procedure and matters of policy, but all must agree on the Senate's high purpose. "This house," he says, "is a sanctuary, a citadel of law, of order, and of liberty. It is here, it is here in this exalted refuge, here if anywhere, that resistance will be made to the storms of political frenzy and the silent arts of corruption." He bids the members farewell. "Though we separate, we will be engaged in the common cause of disseminating the principles of freedom and social order."

Some senators weep; others shake Burr's hand and clap him on the back. The house resolves unanimously to tender its thanks and entire approbation to its retiring president for the impartiality, dignity and ability with which he has fulfilled his duties.

17

He has nowhere to go but west. His creditors, fearing that a defeated politician with famous blood on his hands will attract little law business, force the sale of Richmond Hill. The transaction nets twenty-five thousand dollars, which falls far short of covering his debts. To return to New York risks lawsuits, perhaps debtors' prison.

To stay in Washington is even less feasible. The capital city is a caravansary, a stopover for those dispatched to do the people's business. He has no such business any longer. Jefferson is polite but chilly; other Republicans take their cue from the president. The Federalists would hang him if they could.

To travel south might sully Theo's standing. Her friends would welcome him not simply as her father but also as the slayer of the hated Hamilton. Yet he won't hazard her reputation by bringing his own obloquy near.

So he turns his face toward the mountains and beyond, as his countrymen have done for centuries. The West is the land of opportunity in part because it is the land of forgiveness. Eastern prosecutors rarely pursue their quarry across the mountains, and western etiquette precludes excessive questioning of eastern antecedents or reasons for migrating. In Burr's case, he knows that the death of the haughty Hamilton strikes many westerners as a blow for democracy: for government *by* the people, not merely *of* the people. Democracy is further advanced in the egalitarian West than in the stratified East; the slayer of Hamilton can expect to find friends there.

"The plan of summer operations is to go from Philadelphia to Fort Pitt (Pittsburg)," he writes Theo. "Thence through the states on each side of the Ohio. To visit St. Louis and the mouth of the Missouri; thence through Tennessee (where pass a month) to Orleans." He understands that she frets for his future, after the reverses he has suffered; he assures her that things will work out. "This tour has other objects than mere curiosity—an operation of business, which promises to render the tour both useful and agreeable." He may speculate in land, an occupation ubiquitous in the West and one that has created more fortunes for the canny than all others combined. He may seek a position in the territorial government of Louisiana. "Just at the moment of writing the last word I receive a message from the president informing me that Dr. Browne may have the office of secretary of the government of Louisiana (which means the upper district, whereof St. Louis is the capital). General Wilkinson is appointed governor of that territory." Burr has heard encouraging reports about St. Louis. "It contains about two hundred houses, and some very wealthy people. The inhabitants are French; retain the French manners of the last century; are said to be hospitable; gay to dissipation; the society polished and fashionable. All accounts represent the country as remarkably healthy, fertile, and beautiful. The salary of secretary is, I think, but eight hundred dollars per annum. Certain contingences, however, will make it worth about double that sum. Wilkinson and Browne will suit most admirably as eaters and laughers, and, I believe, in all other particulars."

He worries less for himself than for Theo. "I contemplate the tour with gayety and cheerfulness," he writes her. "The most weighty solicitude on my mind is your health and that of your boy." Northerners often suffer on moving to the South; Theo certainly has. She survives the Carolina winters well enough, but summers bring their variety of complaints. Burr has researched remedies, and he shares the results with his daughter. "You will want stimulus of some kind. For this purpose something is used in all warm countries. In the West Indies they drink rum and they die. In the East Indies and China, ginseng is the panacea. Try ginseng. Some decoction or (bitter) infusion. When my stomach is out of order or wants tone, nothing serves so effectually as a cup of chamomile tea, without sugar or milk. I think this would give you an appetite. Make the experiment. Bathing in seawater is a grand preservative. If your bath be in the house, the best time is an hour or two before dinner. Tepid bath; none of your cold baths for such a machine as yours. If you have no convenience for a warm bath in the house, set a mason to work to-morrow and make one in each of your country houses. It is a high evidence of the barbarism of our Southern states that, in an extent of three hundred miles, filled with wealthy people, and in a hot climate, there should not be, in any one private family, a convenient bathing-room."

He sets off in early April and reaches Pittsburgh at month's end. Boatwrights have been working per orders he has sent ahead; the craft greets its master. "My boat is, properly speaking, a floating house," he tells Theo. "Sixty feet by fourteen, containing dining-room, kitchen with fireplace, and two bedrooms; roofed from stem to stern; steps to go up, and a walk on the top the whole length; glass windows, &c. This edifice costs one hundred and thirty-three dollars, and how it can be made for that sum passes my comprehension."

The boat becomes his base for the next several weeks. It drifts down the Ohio, moved by nothing but the spring-time current and occasional nudges from the boatmen's poles. A skiff carries Burr to shore, letting him walk around Wheeling, Virginia—"a pretty, neat village, well situated on the south bank, containing sixty or eighty houses, some of brick, and some of a fine free stone found in the vicinity," he writes. "Saw several well-dressed women, who had the air of fashion and movements of *vous autres* on the coast." He samples the archaeology of the region near Marietta, Ohio. "We have been walking several miles to see the mounds, parapets, squares, and other remains of unknown antiquity which are found in this neighbourhood," he tells Theo. "I am astonished and confounded; totally unsatisfied with the conjectures of others, and unable to repose on any plausible one of my own." At Cincinnati he meets with fellow veterans of the Revolutionary War; they drink to the memory of General Washington and other departed comrades.

He leaves the "ark," as he has christened the boat, at the Falls of the Ohio, where the town of Louisville is growing up. While the boatmen maneuver the craft around the falls, he travels overland to Lexington and Frankfort before entering Tennessee. Near Nashville he visits the plantation home of Andrew Jackson, the rising star of Tennessee politics, a man who, like most westerners, has nothing against dueling and applauds the demise of Hamilton. "I have been received with much hospitality and kindness, and could stay a month with pleasure," Burr writes Theo. But he presses on, accepting Jackson's offer of a small boat that carries him down the Cumberland to its junction with the Ohio, where the ark is waiting.

Good luck, apparently, causes his path to cross that of James Wilkinson, who is traveling to St. Louis. Wilkinson is a legend in the West, but not all who know him agree on the particulars or significance of the legend. A year younger than Burr, he served with Benedict Arnold during the Revolutionary War, and though he eschewed Arnold's treason he tested the patience of some other superiors until he was forced to resign. After the war he went west to Kentucky and then Louisiana, when the latter was Spanish territory. He developed close ties to Spanish officials at New Orleans—so close, some said, as to cast doubt upon his loyalty to the United States, even after

Spain relinquished Louisiana to France, which sold it to the United States. Then and now Wilkinson has always seemed to have great plans, without revealing what those plans comprise. To Burr in 1805 he is most helpful. "The general and his officers fitted me out with an elegant barge, sails, colours, and ten oars, with a sergeant, and ten able, faithful hands," Burr tells Theo.

The Ohio enters the Mississippi and the ark heads more directly south. "Natchez is a town of three or four hundred houses; the inhabitants traders and mechanics, but surrounded by wealthy planters, among whom I have been entertained with great hospitality and taste," Burr writes Theo. "These planters are, many of them, men of education and refinement; live as well as yours, and have generally better houses. We are now going through a settled country, and, during the residue of my voyage to Orleans, about three hundred miles, I shall take breakfast and dinner each day at the house of some gentleman on shore. I take no letters of introduction; but, whenever I hear of any gentleman whose acquaintance or hospitalities I should desire, I send word that I am coming to see him, and have always met a most cordial reception."

New Orleans is equally hospitable. "This city is larger than I expected, and there are found many more than would be supposed living in handsome style. They are cheerful, gay, and easy." Even the least likely go out of their way. "The mark of attention with which I have been most flattered is a letter from the holy sisters, the Ursuline nuns, congratulating me on my arrival. Having returned a polite answer to this letter, it was intimated to me that the saints had a desire to see me. The bishop conducted me to the cloister. We conversed at first through the grates; but presently I was admitted within, and I passed an hour with them greatly to my satisfaction. None of that calm monotony which I expected. All was gayety, wit, and sprightliness. Saint A. is a very accomplished lady—in manners and appearance a good deal like Mrs. Merry"—the wife of the British minister in Washington, whom Theo knows. "All, except two, appear to be past thirty. They were dressed with perfect neatness; their veils thrown back. We had a repast of wine, fruit, and cakes. I was conducted to every part of the building. All is neatness, simplicity, and order. At parting, I asked them to remember me in their prayers, which they all promised with great promptness and courtesy—Saint A. with earnestness."

Burr is as pleased with the residents of New Orleans as they are with him, and he thinks he could take up residence if the city were not so far from where Theo and young Aaron live. "These will control my fate," he says of the two. He conducts a thorough reconnaissance of the area and several more interviews with the leading men and women. They talk of border troubles with the Spanish, who still control Florida and Texas, and where these troubles might lead. He inquires of the prospects for speculation in land. After three weeks he turns his face finally back toward the East.

As he does he is reminded of the cardinal fact of western geography: that once travelers and emigrants from the

East cross the Allegheny Mountains, gravity pulls them inexorably west and south. New Orleans commands the entire valley of the Mississippi and Ohio, clear to Pittsburgh. Traffic of persons and cargo flows effortlessly down the river to the city near its mouth. Threads of sentiment and patriotism knit the western states to the eastern part of the Union, but stouter cords of physics and commerce bind the western states to one another and perhaps to territory still farther west.

Burr has to fight gravity and perhaps destiny the whole way back east. Travelers going east and north avoid the rivers, with their westerly and southerly currents and winding courses. Many attempt the Natchez Trace, the overland shortcut from Natchez to Nashville. *Trace* is the frontier term for trail, and Burr finds it appropriate. "On the map you will see laid down a road from Nashville to Natchez as having been cut by the order of the minister of war," he writes Theo. "This is imaginary; there is no such road." But there is the trail, which has to suffice.

Its five hundred miles test the stamina of any traveler, and Burr takes time to recuperate at its northern terminus even as he improves previous acquaintances. "For a week I have been lounging at the house of General Jackson, once a lawyer, after a judge, now a planter; a man of intelligence, and one of those prompt, frank, ardent souls whom I love to meet," he tells Theo. "The general has no children, but two lovely nieces made a visit of some days, contributed greatly to my amusement, and have cured me of all the evils of my wilderness jaunt."

Jackson and the other principal men of Nashville throw

a dinner for Burr—"given not to the vice-president," he tells Theo, "but to A.B." Those present concur that the West counts insufficiently in the councils of American national politics; some wonder whether it will ever receive its due. Nearly all despise the Spanish as monarchists, Catholics and a hindrance to expansion; many endorse military measures to oust the "dons" from North American soil.

Burr rides north to Kentucky, where he meets a young man of talent and ambition named Henry Clay. He turns west again, to St. Louis, for a longer meeting with General Wilkinson, who joins Jackson and the other westerners in believing that a war against Spain ought to be waged, and soon.

A long horseback journey returns him to Washington in November. Jefferson's fascination with the West has prompted him to send Meriwether Lewis and William Clark to the Pacific; the explorers and their expedition have subsequently fallen off the map and haven't been heard from in over a year—which makes Jefferson the more curious to learn what Burr thinks of the West. The president and the former vice president spend two days at the executive mansion discussing what Burr has discovered of the region beyond the mountains. The cordiality of the conversation can't disguise the distrust each feels for the other. Jefferson assumes Burr is plotting something and wonders what; Burr believes Jefferson wishes to complete the ruin he has laid for him thus far.

18

With no home, Burr has to keep moving. He has survived on the kindness of strangers for a year; now he seeks the fondness of family. He joins Theo in South Carolina. He tells her and Alston of the wonders of the West and says a man might build a new life there. He doesn't detail his plans, for they haven't congealed into a form he can count on. But he imagines himself a great man in that rising country, and his vision makes Theo admire him more than ever.

He spends the late winter and spring of 1806 shuttling between Washington and Philadelphia. The latter city was the nation's political capital during the 1790s; it remains the country's financial capital, and along Chestnut Street and lesser thoroughfares Burr pursues financial support for the project he is gradually putting together. He raises forty thousand dollars to purchase a large tract of land on the Washita River in Louisiana Territory, convincing the investors they've made a sharp speculation. Other funds outfit an expeditionary force comprising boats, firearms and provisions. What the purpose of the expeditionary force might be, Burr declines to say, at least for the record. Quite possibly he doesn't know himself, not in detail. But the borderlands between the United States and the Spanish holdings in Mexico and Florida are chronically turbulent, with outlaws and raiders crossing in both directions, and turbulence affords opportunity to men of ambition and backing. Till lately Burr's ambition has been political, but the Hamilton duel and his falling-out with Jefferson have closed that route. His backing is building; with money, men and arms at his disposal he might become a national hero—if not to the nation he helped create in the Revolutionary War, then perhaps to some newly formed one.

Burr hints at his plan to men with experience of war. Thomas Truxton commanded privateers during the Revolution; the success of his licensed raiding vessels vaulted him to a captaincy in the regular navy. He climbed to commodore and subsequently smashed the French in the undeclared naval war of 1798. But he bickered with his civilian superiors and resigned in a dispute over rank. He still bristles at Jefferson and the Republican administration.

William Eaton distinguished himself leading a band of mercenaries in the lately ended Barbary Wars against North African pirate principalities. Like Truxton, Eaton was a hero of the rank and file and a thorn to the administration. His irregulars required compensation, for which he applied to the government in Washington, but his claim for reimbursement was rejected. Like Truxton, he feels ill used.

Burr also talks to Anthony Merry, the British minister at Washington. They speak of the state of the hemisphere, of the slipping hold of Spain on Florida and Mexico, of the ambitions of France in the Caribbean, of the manner in which Americans and Britons might constructively collaborate against the Latin powers. Merry is pleased at Burr's approach, not least since Jefferson and the secretary of state, Madison, make Britain their whipping boy in matters political and diplomatic.

By August Burr has accomplished all he can in the East. With a small entourage he sets out again for the West.

19

Theo goes with him. Her husband might join her later—but then again he might not. Stories have circulated of difficulties between Theo and Alston. As with most such stories it is impossible for outsiders to know the truth in the tales, but some suggest cruelty on Alston's part, others an unwillingness in Theo to place her husband ahead of her father in her affections. It must grate on Alston that their son is named for *her* father rather than for his; the boy will grow up a Burr, before an Alston, if she has her way. Her father needs her, she doubtless tells Alston as she heads north to meet him. And she needs him, Alston certainly thinks as he bids her farewell.

Once more Burr drifts down the Ohio, but this time Theo stands beside him. He continues the lessons he has been conducting since her infancy. He points to the places where settlers have cut back the forests and planted crops, and predicts that many more will follow them. He notes the likely locations for villages and towns—some already taken and built on, others striving, still others merely aspirational.

They land at one of the most striving, most aspirational and most unlikely of the new settlements. Blennerhassett Island is a three-mile-long sliver in the Ohio River a bit below the village of Marietta, Ohio. Boatmen and hunters have long visited the island, which splits the river into two narrow channels, but not until the arrival of Harman Blennerhassett in 1798 did anyone think to make it a permanent home. Certainly no one thought to make it such a home as Blennerhassett proceeded to build on the island. Blennerhassett is an Anglicized member of the Irish gentry who got caught on the wrong side of the nationalist troubles of 1798 and decamped to America. He arrived with dreams of Eden, which he sought to implement on the wilderness island to which he gave his name. He built a curiously semicircular mansion surrounded by lawns and gardens that attempted to improve on nature's arrangements; visitors differed as to the extent of his success, as well as on the attractiveness of the house.

The master of the island was away when Burr made his initial reconnaissance, but Burr met and charmed Mrs. Blennerhassett and has subsequently corresponded with her husband. Burr intimates that Blennerhassett's gifts might yield more to their possessor in pursuits beyond his little island. The North American West is not too grand a stage for him. Burr echoes the western sentiment that war with Spain is inevitable and desirable, and he hints that the treasures of Mexico are available for taking by the bold.

Blennerhassett is flattered that such a great man as Burr

thinks well of his prospects. "I hope, sir, you will not regard it indelicate in me to observe to you how highly I should be honored in being associated with you," he writes. "Viewing the probability of a rupture with Spain and the claim for action the country will make upon your talents in the event of an engagement against, or subjugative of, any of the Spanish Territories, I am disposed in the confidential spirit of this letter to offer you my friends and my own services to cooperate in any contemplated measures in which you may embark."

Theo becomes enchanted with Blennerhassett Island. Mrs. Blennerhassett is as much younger than her husband as Theo is than Burr; the two women become fast friends, while little Aaron toddles about the house and grounds, amusing the servants, vexing the pets, alarming his mother and gratifying his grandfather.

Blennerhassett joins Burr in preparing the expeditionary force for a journey downstream. Burr has contracted at Marietta for the construction of fifteen flat-bottomed boats—bateaux, after the French design and nomenclature—and a large keel boat. The bateaux collectively can accommodate five hundred men and their arms and provisions. On the island itself, workers construct kilns for drying and preserving corn. Pigs are slaughtered and their flesh salted and packed into barrels. Wheat is ground into flour and bagged.

Burr meanwhile recruits volunteers for the expedition. He begins with the local militia, who have heard of his service during the Revolutionary War and who respect

Aaron Burr in his enigmatic prime

Theodosia Burr Alston,
her father's darling, pupil and confidante

Richmond Hill, where young Theo astonished
New York with her maturity and grace

The 1800 electoral tally that started the troubles

Alexander Hamilton,
Burr's all-too-mortal enemy

Weehawken, New Jersey, where the fatal duel took place

Andrew Jackson, who hosted Burr in Tennessee

Thomas Jefferson, who determined to crush Burr

James Wilkinson, Burr's accuser

John Marshall, Burr's unlikely ally in the treason trial

Older, perhaps wiser, certainly sadder

him the more for his duel with Hamilton. He guarantees each of them one hundred acres of land in the Washita tract, and he suggests that much larger prizes await them in Mexico should war break out.

Blennerhassett talks up the expedition among the influential men of the neighborhood. He recounts the complaints of westerners against the merchants and politicians of the East, and he wonders aloud whether nature dictates an independent destiny for the region. The American colonies severed their ties to Britain when the cost of those ties outweighed the benefits; why shouldn't the West do the same to the East, seize Spanish territory and forge a new nation looking to the setting sun?

Encouraging a separation of the West from the East will get a man into trouble with the national government, which cannot but interpret it as treason; knowing this, Burr is more circumspect than the garrulous Blennerhassett. He lets others' imaginations roam while himself saying little. Yet his military background and the influence in Washington he lets the westerners think he still enjoys—even if, as he intimates, partisan politics keeps the administration from acknowledging him—make his silence more persuasive than any of his words might be.

20

His silence doesn't stop the authorities from taking note of his movements and activities. The gathering of armed men would arouse suspicion in any case; combined with the rumblings of separation it compels government officials to respond. Jefferson in Washington pens a special message to Congress painting the western conspiracy in the darkest colors. He describes the recruiting, provisioning and arming of the group on the Ohio and asserts its dual purposes. "One of these was the severance of the Union of these States by the Alleghany Mountains; the other an attack on Mexico. A third object was provided, merely ostensible, to wit, the settlement of a pretended purchase of a tract of country on the Washita." The Washita settlement was a ruse to entice the unwitting persons drawn into the plot, Jefferson says.

And the evil genius who conceived the objects of the expedition and set the dangerous chain of events in motion? "The prime mover in these was Aaron Burr, heretofore distinguished by the favor of his country," the president declares.

Jefferson concedes that what he knows of the plot is compounded from sources individually incomplete and collectively still imperfect. "It is chiefly in the form of letters, often containing such a mixture of rumors, conjectures, and suspicions as renders it difficult to sift out the real facts and unadvisable to hazard more than general outlines, strengthened by concurrent information or the particular credibility of the relator." Prudence dictates discretion in drawing surmises. "In this state of the evidence, delivered sometimes, too, under the restriction of private confidence, neither safety nor justice will permit the exposing names, except that of the principal actor, whose guilt is placed beyond question."

21

With the president proclaiming Burr's unquestionable guilt, subordinate officials of the executive branch swing into action. The federal district attorney at Frankfort, Kentucky, J. H. Daviess, is a Federalist from the days when Hamilton was the rising star of the republic; he is that rare westerner who holds Hamilton's death against Burr. Daviess's personal feelings complement Jefferson's condemnation of Burr, and he brings charges against Burr for preparing to make war on a country—Spain—with which America is at peace.

A grand jury is summoned and witnesses called. Burr, having read about Jefferson's declaration of his guilt, attends the session to rebut the president's charges. He represents himself, with the assistance of Henry Clay, the local favorite. Two of Daviess's key witnesses, doubtless discouraged by the overwhelming popular support for Burr, fail to appear. Twice Daviess tries to obtain an indictment; twice he fails. The second failure is treated by the locals as a vindication of Burr; Frankfort hosts a ball that draws men and women from near and far to shake the hand of the illustrious war hero and former vice president.

Burr travels from Frankfort to Nashville to supervise certain matters relating to the expedition. Word of his courtroom triumph precedes him, and the inhabitants of the Tennessee capital hold another ball in his honor. He thanks the good citizens for their congratulations and employs the opportunity to enlist additional recruits.

While at Nashville he learns that Jefferson has called for his arrest. The president rejects the finding of the Kentucky grand jury; on his own authority he decides that Burr is too dangerous to remain free.

Burr gets wind of the order as soon as Tennessee's governor does, and before the latter—perhaps slowed by sympathy for Burr—can arrest him, Burr disappears down the Cumberland River with two boats and a handful of men.

At the confluence of the Cumberland and the Ohio he makes rendezvous with Blennerhassett, who has effected a similar escape from his island. Their combined party includes thirteen boats and some sixty men.

Burr leads the fleet down the Ohio to the Mississippi and down the Mississippi toward New Orleans. Most of the way he is greeted with the same warmth he elicited the year before; new men answer his summons to glory and join the force.

But his prospects narrow the farther south he goes. Mississippi is a federal territory rather than a state, and its governor owes his position to appointment by Jefferson rather than election by the locals; for this reason, perhaps among others, he vows to stifle the Burr rebellion, as he and the president are calling it. He summons the militia and orders them to intercept Burr's force.

In early 1807 one company of the Mississippi militia creeps up the river toward Burr's camp at Bayou Pierre, near Natchez; a second squadron, mounted on horseback, closes in through the forest. The pursuers greatly outnumber Burr's force, and Burr surrenders himself without a fight. He declares to the attorney general of the territory, who personally directs the arrest, that he has no designs whatsoever upon the interests or security of the United States.

Again he finds himself in court. Again a grand jury is summoned. And again the grand jury, persuaded by Burr's history, demeanor and disavowal of any wrongdoing, refuses to indict him. Beyond this, the jury chides the attorney general for wasting their time and endangering American liberties by persecuting an innocent man. Once more Burr exits the courtroom to a hero's reception.

He thereupon requests a statement from the court that he is free to leave the town. The court refuses, to his surprise. The attorney general evidently plans further action against him.

Boldness has marked Burr's steps till now; it suddenly yields to caution and stealth. Concluding that Jefferson will throw one hurdle after another in his path, he disguises himself as a boatman and slips out of town.

The court convenes the next day, with Burr nowhere to

be seen. The governor publicizes the flight and offers two thousand dollars for the fugitive's capture. The offer meets a mixed response: a few persons share Jefferson's fear of Burr's designs, a larger number are enticed by the money and a still larger portion wish Burr godspeed.

Some in the last category facilitate his flight as he heads east across Mississippi and Alabama in the direction of Spanish Florida, where at Pensacola he hopes to find a British vessel to spirit him away. For weeks he eludes his pursuers, living off the land and local sympathy.

In February he and one of the sympathizers, who acts as a guide, approach the village of Wakefield in southwestern Alabama. Night has fallen and the winter cold keeps everyone indoors. Burr and his companion approach a cabin where a lamp burns in the window. They ask directions to the home of a Major Hinson, a gentleman of the district. Nicholas Perkins, the cabin owner, provides the directions but in doing so detects something amiss. The horse of one of the inquirers is too well bred for the neighborhood and the man's boots too fine.

While Burr and his associate ride toward the Hinson home, Perkins wakens the local sheriff and says that he has just seen the fugitive Burr. The sheriff and Perkins head toward Hinson's place.

Burr and his guide reach Hinson's first. The colonel is gone but his wife lets them in.

The sheriff and Perkins approach the cabin carefully. The sheriff explains that since he knows Mrs. Hinson, he will go forward. Perkins should wait in the woods.

Mrs. Hinson opens the door to the sheriff, who is soon seated with Burr and the other man eating a late supper. Perhaps the sheriff has sympathized with Burr all along; perhaps he is charmed by Burr now. But the result is that he makes no move to arrest him, and when Burr retires for the night, the sheriff lies down before the fire and does the same.

Perkins grows colder in the dark. He mutters to himself against the sheriff until he can stand it no longer. He mounts his horse and rides several miles to federal Fort Stoddard, where Captain Edmund Gaines commands. He tells Gaines that Burr is in the neighborhood and that the sheriff refuses to take action. The republic is in peril; the captain must act.

Gaines, like every other officer in the West, knows that capturing Burr is President Jefferson's priority. He gathers a company of dragoons and all set off at a gallop.

Divining Burr's direction, they head for the Pensacola road. An hour after sunrise they spot Burr and his guide in the distance. Gaines catches him ahead of the others. "I presume, sir, that I have the honor of addressing Colonel Burr?" he says.

Burr demands to know under what authority the captain asks the question.

"I am an officer of the army," Gaines replies. "I hold in my hands the proclamations of the president and the governor, directing your arrest."

Burr silently assesses the strength of Gaines's escort and the freshness of their horses and concludes that resistance is futile and escape impossible. With a word he dismisses his guide, whom Gaines allows to leave, and turns his horse to fall in with those of Gaines and the other soldiers.

They ride to Fort Stoddard, where Gaines prepares a company to transport Burr east, per the orders of the president. Meanwhile Burr charms Mrs. Gaines, the other officers' wives and most of the men. He comes near to winning over Gaines himself, but the captain refuses to let personal inclination trump his professional judgment. After two weeks, when Burr's escort of guards is ready, everyone gathers at the gates of the fort to watch the prisoner leave. The ladies wave fondly; some wipe tears from their eyes. Gaines sighs with relief at being rid of the prisoner.

The guard company is headed by Perkins, who vows to see Burr delivered to justice. For two weeks they ride through the wilderness of southern Alabama. Late-winter rains drench the party; wolves howl at night; Indians shadow them during the day. They sleep on the ground and eat the rudest fare. But Burr never complains or displays the slightest discomfort. He is the first to rise each morning and assists the others in making ready. His good humor and solicitude gradually softens their hearts—as Perkins has feared. Perkins warns them all against Burr's wiles, yet he can do little but threaten loss of pay if they let him escape.

Perkins's worries intensify as the party enters South Carolina, which he knows to be the home of Burr's daughter and son-in-law. Perkins takes pains to avoid stopping in settlements, and as the single track of the wilderness gives way to a rutted road, he purchases a carriage in which he compels Burr to ride, with the window shades pulled tight. This tactic sufficiently insulates Burr from the populace, and from his guards, that after a final week of long days crossing North Carolina and southern Virginia, they arrive at Richmond on March 26.

22

Burr's first act on arrival is to pen a note to Theo, who took leave from him on the Ohio and has returned to South Carolina. "It seems that here the business is to be tried and concluded," he writes. "I am to be surrendered to the civil authority tomorrow, when the question of bail is to be determined. In the meantime I remain at the Eagle Tavern." He tells her not to worry. He reminds her of the lessons of her youth. "You have read to very little purpose if you have not remarked that such things happen in all democratic governments. Was there in Greece or Rome a man of virtue and independence, and supposed to possess great talents, who was not the subjective of vindictive and unrelenting persecution?" He jokingly sets her an exercise: "Madame, I pray you to amuse yourself by collecting and collating all the instances to be found in ancient history, which you may connect together, if you please, in an essay, with reflections, comments, and applications. . . . I promise myself great pleasure in the perusal, and I promise you great satisfaction and consolation in the composition."

But Theo isn't consoled, nor is she satisfied to remain at a distance while her father is in peril. She insists on traveling to Richmond, despite the doubts of her husband, who fears for his own political future and anyway wonders if her presence will help or hurt her father's defense. Theo dismisses Alston's concerns and heads north; he tags along to keep her company and limit the damage to his reputation.

23

The Burr trial arrests the attention of the whole country. The alleged crime could not be darker: treason against the American republic. Two decades after the drafting of the Constitution, the republican experiment remains as unfinished and its outcome as uncertain as ever. Skeptics have consistently alleged that a republican form of government suits only small countries; any country as large as the United States will fly apart sooner or later. The contours of American geography—the transit-impeding mountain chain, the west-flowing Ohio River and the Gulf of Mexico–bound Mississippi—add to the ungainliness of the republic. Burr is charged with fomenting the separatism that Americans have long feared.

The stakes could not be higher. Treason is a capital offense; Burr may die if found guilty. The federal government will score a signal victory if Burr is convicted, and the victory will translate into credibility for federal authority generally. Jefferson's reputation will be enhanced at a time when the president is trying to establish a Republican dynasty. A verdict of not guilty, by contrast, will spare Burr, obviously, and embarrass Jefferson.

The participants could not be more illustrious. The defendant is a Revolutionary War hero who has held the second-highest office in the land. His counsel includes Edmund Randolph, formerly a member of the Continental Congress, a framer of the Constitution, attorney general and governor of Virginia, attorney general and secretary of state of the United States; Luther Martin of Maryland, widely considered the most formidable trial lawyer of the age; Charles Lee, another former attorney general of the United States; John Wickham, reputed to be the best lawyer in Virginia, known for ingenuity in argument and wit in presentation; Benjamin Botts, young but already renowned for agility in court; and Burr himself, whose facile intellect and pleasing manner have made him a favorite of juries for decades.

The prosecution is headed by George Hay, an ardent Republican commanding not just the ordinary resources of a district attorney but the vigorous backing of Jefferson, who has made clear he wants Burr's head on a platter. Assisting Hay are William Wirt, the most respected member of the Richmond bar, seconding Hay at the specific request of Jefferson, and Alexander MacRae, the lieutenant governor of Virginia.

The judge is the emerging giant of American jurisprudence: John Marshall. Supreme Court justices still ride the circuit, and Marshall regularly hears cases in his hometown of Richmond. After the defeat of Adams in 1800 by Jefferson and the killing of Hamilton by Burr in 1804, the defense of Federalist principles has fallen to

Marshall, whose energy and success in that cause make him obnoxious to Jefferson. With Marshall in the judge's chair, the Burr trial becomes not simply a matter of treason, as if this were not enough, but a proxy struggle of philosophies of government.

The proceedings begin with the summoning of a grand jury. Among those called are several of the most eminent citizens of Virginia not already involved in the case. William Giles has been a member of the Virginia assembly and senate, governor of the commonwealth and a member of the federal House and Senate. He is a close friend and strong supporter of Jefferson.

For this reason his seating on the grand jury is opposed by Burr. The defendant surprises the court by challenging prospective grand jurors, in the manner that prospective trial jurors have long been challenged. The prosecution objects, but John Marshall lets Burr proceed. Burr adduces evidence that Giles has already made up his mind in the case, prejudging the defendant guilty. Marshall concurs and Giles is dismissed.

Burr similarly succeeds in barring Wilson Cary Nicholas, who crossed swords with Burr when Burr presided over the Senate. Nicholas has loudly proclaimed Burr's guilt in the present case, and he too is sent home.

But eventually the grand jury is seated, and Marshall issues its charge: "To you by the constitution and laws of our country is confided the important right of accusing those whose offenses shall have rendered them subject to punishment under the laws of the United States. It is on you that the fundamental principles on which the stability of our political institutions and the safety of institutions most greatly depend." Justice and the law, alone, must guide the grand jury's actions. "Juries, gentlemen, as well as judges, should be superior to every temptation which hope, fear, or compassion may suggest; who will allow no influence to balance their love of justice; who will follow no guide but the laws of their country."

The grand jury may indict the defendant on any of several charges, Marshall says. But one stands out. "The first on the calendar, as well as the highest known atrocity, is treason against the United States. With a jealousy peculiar to themselves, the American people have withdrawn the subject from the power of their legislature and have declared in their constitution that 'treason against the United States shall consist only in levying war against them, or in adhering to their enemies, giving them aid and comfort.'"

The grand jury accepts Marshall's charge and retires for the day, whereupon Burr steps forward to request that certain evidence gathered by the prosecution be excluded. The authority of the evidence is open to doubt, he says, and the defense has had no chance to examine it. A countermotion by the prosecution to allow the evidence elicits a further objection by the defense, that the prosecution is selectively leaking the evidence to the newspapers. "The press from one end of the continent to the other has been enlisted on their side to excite prejudice against Colonel Burr," John Wickham indignantly declares for Burr.

The prosecution's William Wirt leaps to rebut. "If Aaron Burr be innocent," he says, "instead of resisting this motion he ought to hail it with triumph and exultation. What is it that we propose to introduce? Not the rumors that are floating through the world, nor the bulk of the multitude, nor the speculations of newspapers, but the *evidence of facts*. We propose that the whole evidence, exculpatory as well as accusative, shall come before you; instead of inciting, this is the true mode of correcting prejudices. The world, which it is said has been misled and influenced by falsehood, will now hear the truth. Let the truth come out; let us know how much of what we have heard is false, how much of it is true; how much of what we feel is prejudice, how much of it is justified by fact. Whoever before heard of such an apprehension as that which is professed by the other side? *Prejudice excited by evidence!* Evidence, sir, is the great corrector of prejudice. Why then does Aaron Burr shrink from it?"

Wirt notes that the defense has complained that the prosecution is driven by partisanship. One would expect such a strategy from Burr and his hirelings, he declares. "They would convert the judicial inquiry into a political question; they would make it a question between Thomas Jefferson and Aaron Burr. The purpose is well understood, sir. But it shall not be served." The business of the court is quite different. "We have an account to settle not between Aaron Burr and Thomas Jefferson, but between Aaron Burr and the laws of his country."

Burr himself opposes Wirt. "The question in the present case," he says, "is whether there is probable cause of guilt, and whether time ought to be allowed to collect testimony against me. This time ought generally to be limited; but there is no precise standard on the subject, and much is, of course, left to the sound discretion of the court." Burr hopes the court will note the time already given to the government to prepare its case. "Five months ago a high authority"—Jefferson, though Burr doesn't name him now—"declared that there was a crime, that I was at the head of it; and it mentioned the very place, too, where the crime was in a state of preparation." Surely five months is sufficient to gather evidence. Yet the prosecution is asking for more time.

As to the politics of the case, Burr says, the administration politicized matters from the start. But even if it had not, the defense has every right to challenge its motives. "Surely it is an established principle, sir, that no government is so high as to be beyond the reach of criticism. And it is more particularly laid down that this vigilance is more peculiarly necessary when any government initiates a prosecution; and one reason is on account of the vast disproportion of means which exists between it and the accused. If ever there was a case which justified this vigilance, it is certainly the present one, when the government has displayed such uncommon activity." Burr points out that many of his friends have been seized by the military—"a practice truly consonant with European despotisms." These persons have been compelled to testify against him. His papers have been seized. His mails have been intercepted and opened. An order was issued to kill him if he could not be arrested.

Burr lampoons Jefferson's assertions regarding the peril the country faces on account of the alleged conspiracy. "Our president is a lawyer, and a great one, too. He certainly ought to know what it is that constitutes a war. Six months ago he proclaimed that there was a civil war. And yet for six months they have been hunting for it, and still cannot find one spot where it existed. There was, to be sure, a most terrible war—in the newspapers, but nowhere else."

Amid the reciprocal declamations, the evidence issue centers on a deposition by James Wilkinson. The Louisiana governor was one of the first to alert Jefferson to Burr's activities in the West, and although he is said to have left St. Louis some time earlier, he has yet to arrive in Richmond. The prosecution wishes to admit his written statement; the defense wants to exclude it.

Benjamin Botts puts the issue in constitutional and historical perspective. The defense attorney asks the court to consider the definition of treason. "First," he says, "it must be proved there was an actual war. A war consists wholly in acts, and not in intentions. The acts must in themselves be acts of war; and if they be not intrinsically so, words or intentions cannot make them so. In England, when conspiring the death of the king was treason, the *quo animo* formed the essence of the offense; but in America, the national convention has confined treason to the act. . . . An intention to levy war is not evidence that war was levied. .... Secondly, the war must not only have been levied, but Colonel Burr must be proved to have committed an overt act of treason in that war. A treasonable intention to cooperate is no evidence of actual cooperation. The acts of others, even if in pursuance of his plan, would be no evidence against him. It might not be necessary that he should be present, perhaps; but he must be, at the time of levying the war, cooperating by acts, or, in the language of the Constitution, be committing overt acts. Thirdly, the overt act by the accused, as an actual war, must not only be proved, but it must be proved to have been committed within this district. Fourthly, the overt act must be proved by two witnesses."

John Marshall listens carefully to Botts's disquisition. As the defense counsel closes, the chief justice affirms that Botts has framed the case correctly.

Marshall's assent encourages Burr to make an ambitious request. He asks the court to require President Jefferson to produce certain documents that might assist the defense. The most important such document is a letter from Wilkinson to Jefferson dated October 21, 1806. The president referred to this letter in his special message to Congress. Burr requests as well copies of the reply Jefferson sent to Wilkinson and of the order the president issued to officers of the army and navy near New Orleans.

Luther Martin explains the reasoning of the defense regarding these documents. It is a general principle of the law, Martin says, that an accused person has the right to defend himself; the documents the defendant has requested are essential to an effective defense. Moreover, the documents in question—most notably the president's order to the army and navy—will reveal the motive of the administration in prosecuting the defendant. "We intend to show that by this particular order his property and person were to be destroyed; yes, by these tyrannical orders the life and property of an innocent man were to be exposed to destruction." Jefferson has put a heavy thumb on the scales of justice. "The President has undertaken to prejudge this trial by declaring that of his guilt there can be no doubt. He has assumed to himself the knowledge of the Supreme Being himself, and pretended to search the heart of my highly respected friend. . . . He has let slip the dogs of war, the hell-hounds of destruction, to hunt down my friend. And would this President of the United States, who has raised all of this absurd clamor, pretend to keep back the papers which are wanted for this trial, where life is at stake? It is a sacred principle that in all such cases, the accused has a right to all the evidence which is necessary to his defense. And whoever withholds, willfully, information that would save the life of a person charged with a capital offense is substantially a murderer, and so recorded in the registry of Heaven."

William Wirt states his astonishment that Martin is resorting to such ad hominem arguments. "I cannot take my seat, sir," the associate prosecutor says, "without expressing my deep and sincere sorrow at the policy which the gentlemen in the defense have thought it necessary to adopt." To whom do they address these ludicrous remarks—

"these perpetual philippics"—against the administration? "Do they flatter themselves that this court feel political prejudices which will supply the place of argument and innocence on the part of the prisoner? Their conduct amounts to an insinuation of the sort. But I do not believe it. . . . Or is it on the bystanders that the gentlemen expect to make a favourable impression? And do they use the court merely as a canal through which they may pour upon the world their undeserved invectives against the government? Do they wish to divide the popular resentment and diminish thereby their own quota? Before the gentlemen arraign the administration, let them clear the skirts of their client. Let them prove his innocence. . . . I hope that the court, for their own sakes, will compel a decent respect to that government of which they themselves form a branch. On our part, we wish only a fair trial of this case. If the man be innocent, in the name of God let him go. But while we are on this question of his guilt or innocence, let us not suffer our attention and judgment to be diverted and distracted by the introduction of other subjects foreign to the inquiry."

Marshall lets the two sides contend at length; only on the fifth day does he deliver his judgment. The president must surrender the documents the defense requires. The president is not above the law, Marshall says. Conceivably the president could contend that providing such evidence would fatally impair his ability to fulfill the duties of his office. But such impairment is unlikely, and in any event responsibility rests with the executive branch to demonstrate it, not with the judicial branch to infer it.

The members of the prosecution are disappointed at Marshall's decision; they soon learn that Jefferson is livid. Hay receives a scorching letter from the White House. "Shall we move to commit Luther Martin as *particeps criminis* with Burr?" Jefferson writes. He threatens to turn his best investigator loose on Martin. "His evidence will pull down this unprincipled and impudent Federalist bulldog, and add another proof that the most clamorous defenders of Burr are all his accomplices."

But Jefferson has no answer to Marshall, and he grumblingly turns over the documents Burr has demanded.

24

The proceedings take a dramatic turn when James Wilkinson abruptly appears. The general and governor is the prosecution's key witness; to him, it claims, Burr revealed his plans for capturing New Orleans with his expeditionary force and turning the Mississippi Valley against the government in Washington. Wilkinson knows so much, the prosecution explains, because Burr wanted him to be part of the conspiracy. They communicated in cipher, which makes the correspondence all the more incriminating. With Wilkinson in Richmond, the prosecution believes its case is made.

Perhaps Burr does too. Washington Irving has joined the defense team, not yet having shifted his full energies from law to literature. He paints the moment at which the prisoner and his accuser meet in the courtroom: "Burr was seated with his back to the entrance, facing the judges, and conversing with one of his counsel when Wilkinson strutted into the court and took a stand in a parallel line with Burr on his right hand. Here he stood for a moment swelling like a turkey cock, and bracing himself up for the encounter of Burr's eyes. The latter did not take any notice of him until the judge directed the clerk to swear General Wilkinson; at the mention of the name Burr turned his head, looked him full in the face with one of his piercing regards, swept his eye over his whole person from head to foot, as if to scan its dimensions and then coolly resumed his former position, and went on conversing with his counsel as tranquilly as ever. The whole look was over in an instant, but it was an admirable one. There was no appearance of study or constraint in it; no affectation of disdain or defiance; a slight expression of contempt played over his countenance, such as you would show on regarding any person to whom you were indifferent, but whom you considered mean and contemptible."

Wilkinson's arrival pushes the proceedings forward; shortly the grand jury, concluding there is enough evidence to go to trial, indicts Burr. The defendant, according to the windy indictment drawn up by the prosecution, "not having the fear of God before his eyes, nor weighing the duty of his said allegiance"—to the United States—"but being moved and seduced by the instigation of the devil, wickedly devising and intending the peace and tranquility of the said United States to disturb and to stir, move and excite insurrection, rebellion and war against the said United States . . . with force and arms unlawfully, falsely, maliciously and traitorously did compass, imagine and intend to raise and levy war, insurrection and rebellion against the said United States," and "with a great multitude of persons whose names are at present unknown . . .

armed and arrayed in a warlike manner, that is to say, with guns, swords, and dirks and other warlike weapons . . . most wickedly did ordain, prepare and levy war against the said United States . . . with the wicked and traitorous intention to descend the said river"—the Ohio—"and the river Mississippi and by force and arms traitorously to take possession of a city commonly called New Orleans."

Upon the reading of the indictment, Marshall asks Burr how he pleads. "I acknowledge myself to be the person named in the indictment," he responds. "I plead not guilty, and put myself upon my country for trial."

25

To this point in the proceedings Burr has been free on bail, and he spends his hours outside the courtroom with Theo, Aaron and Alston. He exhibits his customary aplomb and reassures them that all will end well. Theo displays the confidence she always feels in her father. Alston, aware of the power of the presidency, quietly harbors doubts. Small Aaron is blissfully ignorant of the meaning of the events.

Upon the indictment Marshall determines that Burr needs to be confined. Briefly he allows the prisoner to stay under armed guard in the house rented by his attorney Luther Martin. But he then orders Burr transferred to the local prison, where he occupies a cell on the third floor.

He remains there through the month of July. Marshall has other cases to hear, and the prosecution wants time to perfect its arguments against Burr. The jury phase of Burr's trial is scheduled to begin in early August.

Theo and Aaron help him pass the time, although in the confines of his cell there is only so much they can do. She brings news of the outside world; Burr encourages her continued self-improvement. Father and daughter speak of what Aaron will become.

They try to ignore what may become of Burr. But as the summer heat mounts, as one weary day edges into the next, as they ponder how far he has fallen already, their assurances to each other that everything will come right require greater and greater effort.

26

The trial proper begins at noon on Monday, August 3. Prospective jurors are summoned and examined. "What opinion have you formed of me?" Burr asks one, Jerman Baker.

"A very bad one, which I have expressed often when called upon, and often when not," Baker answers. He is dismissed.

Edward Carrington is a military veteran who admits to having been swayed against Burr by recent reports in the press. Burr inquires: "Have you, Colonel, any prejudice of a more settled kind and ancient date against me?"

"None at all," Carrington replies. He is accepted.

A farmer named Morrison professes no prejudice against Burr. But he remarks that the defense might fear him even so. "My first name is Hamilton." He is rejected.

After an initial display of cooperation, the two sides descend into squabbling over who should be impaneled. They fight over particular individuals, then retreat to higher ground to contest the fundamental principles of trial by jury of one's peers. Marshall lets the lawyers earn their fees before he steps in. Familiarity with the charges against the prisoner, Marshall says, is no ground for disqualification. But strongly held and expressed opinions can be. "To have made up and delivered the opinion that the prisoner entertained the treasonable designs with which he is charged, and that he retained those designs, and was prosecuting them when the act charged in the indictment is alleged to have been committed, is good cause of challenge."

Marshall's directive pushes the selection process to a conclusion, and the argument phase begins. George Hay opens for the prosecution. He addresses the nature and sequence of acts constituting treason. "Gentlemen, common sense and principles founded on considerations of national safety certainly require that the crime of treason should be completed before the actual commission of hostilities against the government," he says. "If force must be employed before treason shall be said to be perpetrated, what is the consequence? Why, that the traitor will so take his steps as not to strike a blow till he be in such an attitude as to be able to bid defiance to the government and laugh at your definitions of treason. If he be a man of common understanding, he will not hazard a blow till his arrangements be so complete that the blow shall be fatal. It will, then, be a matter of very little consequence to him what may be the definition of the crime which he has thus committed. What, then, is the point at which a treasonable conspiracy shall be said to have matured into treason? What shall be said to be an overt act of treason in this country? The answer is this, gentlemen of the jury, that an assemblage of men convened for the purpose of effecting by force a treasonable design, which force is intended to be employed before their dispersion, is treasonable, and the persons engaged in it are traitors." Hay acknowledges that this is not literally what the courts have previously ruled. "But it is substantially the same, and is given in conformity to what I understand to be the spirit of that decision."

Hay proceeds to detail Burr's treasonous plans. "It will be proved to you, gentlemen of the jury, that the design of the prisoner was not only to wage war against the Spanish provinces but to take possession of the City of New Orleans, as preparatory to that design; to detach the people of that country from this, and establish an independent government there, and to dismember the union, separate the western from the eastern states, making the Allegheny Mountains the boundary line. You will perceive from the evidence that he intended to take possession of New Orleans, to excite the people there to insurrection, and to take advantage of the hostile sentiments which prevailed to the west of the Alleghenies against the Spaniards."

Hay allows that Burr did not reveal his entire project to all those he drew into his web. "But he did disclose it to a few; and fortunately for our country he was mistaken in his opinion of those persons in whom he confided." These persons will tell their story, and Burr's, Hay says.

The prosecutor traces Burr's travels during the previous eighteen months. "For the purpose of accomplishing these great designs, of establishing an empire in the West, of which New Orleans was to be the capital, and the accused was to be chief, he made two long visits to the western country. He went to Ohio, Tennessee and Kentucky, in fact to all the western world, and traveled in various directions, till he went finally to New Orleans. Wherever he went, he spoke disrespectfully of the government of his country, with a view to facilitate the consummation of his own designs. He represented it as destitute of energy to support or defend our national rights against foreign enemies, and of spirit to maintain our national character. To those in whom he confided, he asserted that all the men of property and influence were dissatisfied with its arrangements, because they were not in the proper situation to which they were entitled; that with five hundred men he could effect a revolution by which he could send the president to Monticello, intimidate Congress, and take the government into his own hands; that the people of the United States had so little knowledge of their rights, and so little disposition to maintain them, that they would meanly and tamely acquiesce in this shameful usurpation."

Hay details how Burr's treasonous plan took material shape. "In the summer and fall of 1806, men were actually enlisted, boats were built on the waters of the Ohio, provisions purchased to an enormous amount and arms and ammunition provided." The men were promised land in Louisiana, but this was "merely a cover to conceal the real design." Those who knew of the plan against Spain were lulled into complacency. "All were told that the design was just and honorable, known and approved by the government, in which the cooperation of the army was to be expected, in which great wealth was to be acquired, and that it would be developed as soon as the proper time for the disclosure arrived."

That time, however, did not arrive. James Wilkinson, having discerned Burr's designs, rescued the republic. "If he had acted the part of a traitor instead of performing the character of a patriot, I ask: What would have become of this country at this moment? There would have been a civil war waging in the West, and the people of the United States, united as they are by interest, by sympathy and blood, would have been involved in a sanguinary contest, while our eastern coasts would have been insulted and ravaged by an insolent and rapacious foe, in consequence of our divided situation."

Hay asks the jury not to be swayed by the defendant's previous high office. "It is true that the prisoner has been vice president of the United States; he has been the second in office in the government of this country, and perhaps second in the confidence and affection of the people." But this simply aggravates, rather than mitigates, his guilt. "I call upon you, gentlemen of the jury, to disregard all such distinctions in this land of liberty, equality and justice, to view this case in the same light in which you would regard it if any other man in the community were brought before you. I call on you to do justice, and to decide the cause according to the evidence which will be produced before you."

27

Hay scarcely finishes before the defense challenges the weak spot in the prosecution's case. The Burr side's objection takes the form of a challenge to the prosecution's proposed order of examining witnesses, but it goes deeper—to the issue of whether a crime has even been committed. As Luther Martin explains: "The question is, whether the prosecutors must not prove an overt act in the first instance, before any other evidence can be introduced?" The prosecution has put forward an irregular definition of treason, one not approved by the Supreme Court. Before the prosecution begins questioning witnesses, Martin says, it must demonstrate that treason has been committed. "If A were indicted for killing B, would the legal order be to prove, in the first instance, that long and frequent animosities had existed between them? The counsel for the prosecution must first prove that B has been killed by somebody." Likewise in a case of horse-stealing: "Does the public prosecutor go into proof of the felonious intention before proving that the horse has been taken?" Similar logic applies to the present case. "They charge us with having committed treason in 'levying war' against the United States. This charge is too vague, and must be supported by full testimony according to the well known principles of the law. . . . If you should permit the witnesses to go into complicated tales of schemes and plots of severing the union, resting solely on the imputed intentions of the accused, and yet the result of a long and elaborate inquiry would be that there was no act of war, it would be worse than a mere waste of time. . . . Prejudices would be increased; the intention would be taken for the deed, under the influence of impressions not to be resisted when the act was incomplete. The jury ought not to be troubled with evidence which is wholly immaterial till the overt act be proved."

John Marshall ponders the objections of the defense but lets the prosecution call its witnesses. "Levying of war is a fact which must be decided by the jury," he said. The evidence must be heard for the jury to render its decision.

The prosecution summons William Eaton, the controversial hero of the war against the Barbary pirates. "During the winter of 1805–6—I cannot be positive as to the distinct point of time, yet during that winter," Eaton says, "at the city of Washington, Aaron Burr signified to me that he was organizing a military expedition to be moved against the Spanish provinces on the southwestern frontiers of the United States, I understood under the authority of the general government. From our existing controversies with Spain, and from the tenor of the president's communications to both houses of Congress, a conclusion was naturally drawn that war with that power was inevitable. I had just then returned from the coast of Africa, and having been for many years employed on your frontier or on a coast more barbarous and obscure, I was ignorant of the estimation in which Mr. Burr was held by his country. The distinguished rank he held in society and the strong marks of confidence which he had received from his fellow citizens did not permit me to doubt of his patriotism. As a military character, I had been acquainted with none within the United States under whose direction a soldier might with greater security confide his honor than with Mr. Burr. In case of my country's being involved in a war, I should have thought it my duty to obey so honorable a call as was proposed to me. Under impressions like these, I did engage to embark myself in the enterprise, and pledged myself to Mr. Burr's confidence."

Burr showed him maps of Mexico, Eaton says, and other documents pertaining to an invasion of that country. But gradually Eaton divined that more was involved. "From certain indistinct expressions and innuendoes I admitted a strong suspicion that Mr. Burr had other projects. He used strong expressions of reproach against the administration of the government; accused them of want of character, want of energy, and want of gratitude. He seemed desirous of irritating my resentment by dilating on certain injurious strictures I had received on the floor of Congress, on account of certain transactions on the coast of Tripoli, and also on the delays in adjusting my accounts for advances of money on account of the United States."

But Eaton says he kept his doubts to himself. "As I had by this time begun to suspect that the military expedition he had on foot was unlawful, I permitted him to believe myself resigned to his influence, that I might understand the extent and motive of his arrangements."

The ruse worked. "Mr. Burr now laid open his project of revolutionizing the territory west of the Allegheny; establishing an independent empire there; New Orleans to be the capital, and he himself to be the chief; organizing a military force on the waters of the Mississippi and carrying the conquest to Mexico. . . . He proposed to give me a distinguished command in his army; I understood him to say the second command. I asked him who would command in chief. He said, General Wilkinson." Eaton knows Wilkinson and evinced skepticism that he would accept a position inferior to Burr or anyone else. Burr waved away the objection. "From the tenor of much conversation on this subject, I was prevailed upon to believe that the plan of revolution meditated by Mr. Burr and communicated to me had been concerted with General Wilkinson and would have his cooperation, for Mr. Burr repeatedly and very confidently expressed his belief that the influence of General Wilkinson with his army, the promise of double pay and rations, the ambition of his officers and the prospect of plunder and military achievements would bring the army generally into the measure."

Prosecutor Hay asks why Eaton did not share his suspicions with members of the administration.

"The situation which these communications, and the

impressions they made upon me, placed me in was peculiarly delicate," Eaton explains. "I had no overt act to produce against Mr. Burr. He had given me nothing upon paper, nor did I know of any person in the vicinity who had received similar communications and whose testimony might support mine." Moreover, Burr's justifications carried a certain plausibility. "Mr. Burr talked of this revolution as a matter of right, inherent in the people, and constitutional: a revolution which would rather be advantageous than detrimental to the Atlantic states, a revolution which must eventually take place, and for the operation of which the present crisis was peculiarly favorable." Moreover, Eaton says, he feared Burr. "I durst not place my lonely testimony in the balance against the weight of Mr. Burr's character, for by turning the tables upon me, which I thought any man capable of such a project was very capable of doing, I should sink under the weight."

Hay completes the prosecution's questioning of Eaton, and Burr approaches the witness to cross-examine. "You spoke of my revolutionizing the western states," he says. "How did you understand that the union was to be separated?"

"Your principal line was to be drawn by the Allegheny Mountains," Eaton replies. "You were persuaded that you had secured to you the most considerable citizens of Kentucky and Tennessee, but expressed some doubts about Ohio—I well recollect that, on account of the reason which you gave: that they were too much of a plodding, industrial people to engage your enterprise."

"How was the business to be effected?"

"I understood that your agents were in the western country, that the army and the commander in chief were ready to act at your signal, and that these, with the adventurers who would join you, would compel the states to agree to a separation. Indeed, you seemed to consider New Orleans as already yours, and that from this point you would send expeditions into the other provinces, make conquests and consolidate your empire."

Why, again, Burr asks, had Eaton taken no action to oppose this scheme?

"I determined to use you, until I got everything out of you, on the principle that when innocence is in danger, to break faith with a bad man is not fraud but virtue."

28

The next witness is Thomas Truxton, the naval hero. "Have you not had several conversations with the accused about the Mexican expedition?" prosecutor Hay asks.

"About the beginning of the winter of 1805–6 Mr. Burr returned from the western country to Philadelphia," Truxton replies. "He frequently, in conversation with me, mentioned the subject of speculations in western land, opening a canal and building a bridge. Those things were not interesting to me in the least, and I did not pay much attention to them." Burr then changed the subject, Truxton says. "Mr. Burr mentioned to me that the government was weak, and he wished me to get the navy of the United States out of my head; that it would dwindle to nothing, and that he had something to propose to me that was both honorable and profitable. . . . He told me that he wished to see me unwedded from the navy of the United States, and not to think more of those men at Washington; that he wished to see or make me—I do not recollect which of those two terms he used—an admiral; that he contemplated an expedition to Mexico in the event of a war with

Spain, which he thought inevitable. He asked me if Havana could be easily taken in the event of a war. I told him that it would require the cooperation of a naval force. Mr. Burr observed to me that that might be obtained. He asked me if I had any personal knowledge of Carthagena and La Vera Cruz, and what would be the best mode of attacking them by sea and land. I gave him my opinion very freely. Mr. Burr then asked me if I would take command of a naval expedition. I asked him if the executive of the United States were privy to or concerned in the project. He answered emphatically that he was not. . . . I told Mr. Burr that I would have nothing to do with it. . . . He observed to me that in the event of a war, he intended to establish an independent government in Mexico; that Wilkinson, the army and many officers of the navy would join. I told Mr. Burr that I did not see how any officer of the United States could join. He said that General Wilkinson had projected the expedition, and he had matured it; that many greater men than Wilkinson would join, and that thousands to the westward would join."

Truxton says he doubted the premise of Burr's plan. "I told him there would be no war." Burr insisted there would be. "He said, however, that if he was disappointed as to the event of war, he was about to complete a contract for a large quantity of land on the Washita; that he intended to invite his friends to settle it, that in one year he would have a thousand families of respectable and fashionable people, and some of them of considerable property; that it was a fine country, and that they would have a charming society, and in two years he would have doubled the number of settlers. And being on the frontier he would be ready to move whenever a war took place. . . . Mr. Burr said that after the Mexican expedition, he intended to provide a formidable navy, at the head of which he intended to place me; that he intended to establish an independent government and give liberty to an enslaved world."

Burr, cross-examining, asks Truxton to characterize the tone of their conversations. "Was there any reserve on my part?" he inquires.

"We were very intimate," Truxton answers. "There seemed to be no reserve on your part."

"Did you ever hear me express any intention or sentiment respecting a division of the Union?"

"I never heard you speak of a division of the Union."

"Did I not state to you that the Mexican expedition would be very beneficial to this country?"

"You did."

"Had you any serious doubt as to my intentions to settle those lands?"

"So far from that, I was astonished at the intelligence of your views contained in newspapers received from the western country after you went thither."

"Would you not have joined in the expedition if sanctioned by the government?"

"I would most readily get out of my bed at twelve o'clock at night to go in defense of my country at her call, against England, France, Spain or any other country."

Peter Taylor, the prosecution's next witness, was a gardener on Blennerhassett Island. He explains how Harman Blennerhassett boasted of the aims of the military expedition he and Burr were putting in motion. "I will tell you what, Peter, we are going to take Mexico, one of the finest and richest places in the whole world," Taylor quotes him. Taylor adds, "He said that Mr. Burr would be the king of Mexico, and Mrs. Alston, the daughter of Mr. Burr, was to be the queen of Mexico, whenever Mr. Burr died. He said that Mr. Burr had made fortunes for many in his time, but none for himself; but now he was going to make something for himself. He said that he had a great many friends in the Spanish territory; no less than two thousand Roman Catholic priests were engaged, and that all their friends too would join, if once he could get to them; that the Spaniards, like the French, had got dissatisfied with their government and wanted to swap it. He told me that the British were also friends in this piece of business, and that he should go to England, on this piece of business, for Mr. Burr."

Prosecutor Hay asks Taylor about the activities at Blennerhassett's. "Were you not on the island when the people were there?"

"Yes."

"When did the boats leave the island?"

"It was contemplated to sail on the sixth of December, but the boats were not ready. They did not come till the tenth, Sunday. . . . They sailed on the Wednesday night following."

"How many boats were there?"

"Four."

"How many men from the boats came ashore?"

"About thirty."

"What did the men do who did not belong to the boats?"

"Some were packing meat, and some were packing other things."

"Had they any guns?"

"Some of them had; some of the people went a-shooting. But I do not know how many there were."

"What kind of guns—rifles or muskets?"

"I can't tell whether rifles or muskets. I saw no pistols but what belonged to Blennerhassett himself."

"Was there any powder or lead?"

"They had powder, and they had lead both. I saw some powder in a long small barrel, like a churn. But I was so employed I could not notice particularly. Some of the men were engaged in running bullets, but I do not know how many."

"Did you carry some boxes to the boats?"

"I carried half a bushel of candles and some brandy— several boxes—but I knew not what they contained, and a great many things besides, of which I knew nothing."

William Love says much the same thing as Taylor, but neither man can place Burr on the island. Dudley Wood-bridge remembers seeing Burr with Blennerhassett at Marietta when Burr ordered the construction of the boats and the purchase of the provisions.

"Do you recollect that I told you that I wanted the

description of boats used in the Mohawk River?" Burr asks Woodbridge on cross-examination. "And were they not made for shoal water, and to go up the stream?"

"You did. The boats were to be calculated for shallow water."

"You know Mr. Blennerhassett well," Burr says. "Was it not ridiculous for him to be engaged in a military enterprise? How far can he distinguish a man from a horse—ten steps?"

"He is very near-sighted. He cannot know you from any of us, at the distance we are now from one another. He knows nothing of military affairs."

William Wirt, for the prosecution, interrupts: "What were his pecuniary resources? What was the state of his money matters?"

"I believe they were not as great as generally imagined," Woodbridge replies. "His fortune is much less than is generally understood. He has not over five or six thousand dollars in the hands of his agent at Philadelphia. His island and improvements cost about forty or fifty thousand dollars. It would not, however, sell, except to a person of the same cast with Mr. Blennerhassett."

"Is he esteemed a man of vigorous talents?" Wirt inquires.

"He is, and a man of literature. But it was mentioned among the people in the country that he had every kind of sense but common sense."

29

The prosecution is about to summon further witnesses when the defense renews its objection to the order of evidence. More testimony on the events on Blennerhassett Island will illegitimately and irrevocably prejudice the jury, John Wickham declares. "It not only appearing from the proofs, but being distinctly admitted, that the accused, at the period when war is said to have been levied against the United States, was hundreds of miles distant from the scene of action, it becomes necessary for his counsel to object to the introduction of any such testimony, as, according to our view of the law on this subject, it is wholly irrelevant and inadmissible." Wickham surveys the history of England, France and the United States to support his point. "The great object of the American constitution was to perpetuate the liberties of the people of this country. The framers of that instrument well knew the dreadful punishments inflicted, and the grievous oppressions produced, by constructive treasons in other countries." Kings in England made mere dissent a species of treason. Robespierre sent his critics to the guillotine as traitors. The framers of the Constitution insisted on guarding against such excesses. "The language which they have used for this purpose is plain, simple and perspicuous. There is no occasion to resort to the rules of construction to fix its meaning. It explains itself. Treason is to consist in levying war against the United States, and it must be public or open war; two witnesses must prove that there has been an overt act." The prosecution has failed to produce such witnesses or to demonstrate such an overt act. It has adduced evidence that Aaron Burr did not agree with the administration and perhaps envisioned a future for the United States different from the one endorsed by a majority of the American people. But to construe this as treason, as the methods of the prosecution attempt to do, is to pervert the very meaning of the Constitution and of American history. "They have a direct tendency to root out and destroy every principle of freedom. . . . I trust they will never be sanctioned in this country."

John Marshall agrees. On August 31, Marshall delivers a learned and lengthy opinion. He notes that the prosecution has conceded that Burr was not at Blennerhassett Island when the acts described in the indictment took place. He considers what the framers meant when they said, "Treason against the United States shall consist only in levying war against them." Citing additional precedents from English and American law, Marshall asserts that levying war requires "overt acts," not merely the planning or preparation for such acts. Moreover, the Constitution stipulates that these acts be witnessed by two persons.

Circumstantial evidence does not suffice. Of particular significance in the present case: "No testimony relative to the conduct or declarations of the prisoner elsewhere and subsequent to the transaction on Blennerhassett's Island can be admitted, because such testimony, being in its nature merely corroborative and incompetent to prove the overt act itself, is irrelevant until there be proof of the overt act by two witnesses."

With this statement Marshall effectively explodes the case against Burr. The prosecution hasn't produced one witness, let alone two, to any overt acts of war by Burr. Yet the jury must render the final verdict, Marshall says. "The jury have now heard the opinion of the court on the law of the case. They will apply that law to the facts, and will find a verdict of guilty or not guilty as their own consciences may direct."

So instructed, the jury requires little time to deliberate. "We of the jury say that Aaron Burr is not proved to be guilty under this indictment by any evidence submitted to us," the foreman declares. "We therefore find him not guilty."

30

Burr is enough the lawyer to appreciate the historical signifi-
cance of his acquittal, and enough the ironist to relish the
way the decision was reached. Jefferson has long been the
voice of strict construction of the Constitution; with few
exceptions (including the purchase of Louisiana, the territory at the heart of the current controversy) he contends
that what the Constitution does not expressly authorize is
forbidden. The words of the federal charter mean what
they say and nothing more. And yet in the present case
Jefferson and his prosecutors have urged the court to
accept a broad construction of the treason clause, appeal-
ing to an underlying meaning rather than the letter of the
law. On the other side, John Marshall in most matters has
advocated and practiced a generous construction of the
Constitution, allowing the courts latitude in interpreting
the charter and the government energy in pursuing its
goals. Yet Marshall in the present case has insisted on the
letter of the law as it relates to treason and has placed
handcuffs on the government in its prosecution. Burr
understands the power of precedent, and he can guess that

Marshall's handcuffs will stay on government prosecutors for a long time, making treason very difficult to prove in American courts.

But Burr is also enough the realist to recognize that his victory, however politically ironic and legally historic, is personally pyrrhic. He won't be hanged or go to prison on the treason charges, but neither will he resume anything like a normal life. Jefferson has already excommunicated him from the Republican party; angrier than ever, the president will forbid Republicans from engaging Burr even as a lawyer. Nor will the Federalists furnish a refuge; Hamilton's blood has made Burr a pariah for the opposition party as well.

He briefly resumes his law practice, but clients are scarce. As the practice falters, his creditors close in. Prison looms, not for treason but for debt. Having attempted to flee west, unsuccessfully, he turns his face east. He quietly informs Theo, who has returned to South Carolina after accompanying him to New York, that he is departing for Europe. "My letters to you will be often in a strange handwriting, and with various signatures, sometimes feminine," he says. "Put all my papers and manuscript books into some one box (you may get one made for the purpose, if you please), and leave it with Mrs. P., keeping yourself the key. Tell her, in a manner which she may or may not understand, that they are yours." Theo should write to him as G. H. Edwards, the name under which he will travel.

She does so, in sibling guise. "After your departure, my

dear brother, we were alarmed with a report that you had been taken by the French," she says. "But as it was immediately contradicted, I yielded to my belief in the superiority of the English at sea, and to my reliance in the protection of your friend Neptune. I am extremely anxious and impatient to hear from you, and learn the particulars of your voyage. Never were hopes brighter than mine. To look on the gloomy side would be death to me, and without reserve I abandon myself to all the gay security of a sanguine temper. Adieu." She adds: "A. B. A. is well, and kisses you, as does your devotedly affectionate, Mary Ann Edwards."

They share a cipher code for references to friends, lest their letters be read by Jefferson's spies and those friends be compromised. "It was omitted in my last to say that 69 has given me letters to the two principal partners of the house of 70," Burr writes. "69's had not arrived. My health has been improved by the journey. Communicate thus much to 71 and 72."

He lands in London and charms the locals. Jeremy Bentham, the famous utilitarian philosopher and reformer, becomes a confidant and fast friend. Bentham invites Burr to Barrow Green, his summer estate outside London. "Mr. Bentham's countenance has all that character of intense thought which you would expect to find," Burr writes Theo. "But it is impossible to conceive a physiognomy more strongly marked with ingenuousness and philanthropy. He is about sixty, but cheerful even to playfulness." Bentham makes Burr one of his household. "After assigning to me my apartment, he led me immediately into what he calls his 'workshop' (a spacious room, fitted up with great convenience for his purposes), showed me his papers, and gave me an unqualified privilege to read anything and at any time. It was impossible to have given me a more flattering mark of confidence. We pass about six hours a day in our separate rooms, and the residue together—hitherto without ennui. Mr. Bentham loses nothing by being seen and known. I have daily new reason to admire the amazing extent and acuteness of his mind."

Burr tells Bentham of Theo and her intellectual attainments. Bentham, an advocate of women's education, applauds Burr's and Theo's efforts and contributes to them. "Make up, if you can find room, for my dear little Theodosia, a packet of all my combustibles that you can find," he directs Burr: "*Panopticon; Hard-labour Bill; Pelham's Letters and Plea for the Constitution; Poor Management; Judicial Establishment; Political Tactics and Emancipation.*" Some of these works have not been published yet and are available only in pages. "Thus you see you are to possess his works by his own special gift," Burr tells Theo. He adds: "By the next ship, also, I shall send you a bust of Mr. Bentham, a very good representation of him, but has not the force of the original. Still you will admire it; and so you ought, for you may rank him among your admirers."

Transatlantic delivery, however, is uncertain. "Not one word from you has reached me since those few lines from the first stage," Theo writes after several months. "I did not expect to have remained thus long in this painful suspense. There are a thousand vague reports about you. As it regards myself, conjecture on the subject is at a stand, and I write now almost without a hope of being read. I write without pleasure, and only, indeed, to satisfy my desire of seizing every opportunity to gratify you, even though I should have only one chance of success in a million."

Burr replies that the lack of letters is not his fault. "I write you a great deal, but do not choose to trust it to ordinary modes of conveyance. The next safe private hand, you shall have some details. I have on hand (that is, in my head) a stock that will serve you for some years of amusement. I write by this conveyance to 71, whom I must ever recommend to your affection and confidence." He appends a matter of business: "Out of the money which you will receive on 1st December, remit to Jeremy Bentham, for me, two hundred guineas. T. W. Moore will put you in a way to remit with safety and without loss."

Eventually one of his letters gets through. "I cannot tell you what pleasure it gave me to find that you had already introduced me to so great and celebrated a person as Jeremy Bentham," Theo replies. "At such a distance, amid so many new and interesting objects, to think constantly of me; that I should be present to your thoughts, and the subject of your conversations during your first interview with a man so calculated to absorb all your attention, and so likely to converse on things of a very different order from me and my concerns, delights and flatters me really more than I can express."

She relates the most recent news from Washington. "Our politicians and wise ones predict that Madison must be president and the embargo continued." The embargo of America's foreign trade is Jefferson's attempt to halt the seizure of American shipping by the navies of Britain and France as those historic rivals struggle for mastery of Europe. The measure is highly unpopular, especially in the commerce-dependent seaboard states. "The legislature of Connecticut, or, rather, a committee named for the purpose, have framed some very spirited resolutions on the subject of the embargo, protesting against its indefinite continuance as an infringement of the rights of the people. Indeed, from the temper of the Eastern states at present, it is very generally believed that, unless the embargo is raised, rebellion in that part of the Union will take place speedily."

31

Theo's news is vital to Burr. His exile and false identity shield him from his American creditors and meanwhile afford him the opportunity to pursue his western plans, which remain inchoate and opportunistic but which, if successful, will win him the fame to foil his enemies and the fortune to satisfy his creditors. "If I had nothing but amusement in view, this would be my residence for at least six months," he writes Samuel Swartout, an American merchant and fellow western enthusiast then in London, from Bentham's Barrow Green. But he does have more in view. "The key of the drawers which contain my papers is herewith enclosed. Please to select out Gould's *Surveys of the Coast of Florida,* four sheets. A map of North Carolina, four sheets. Map of Mexico, large sheet, manuscript. A map of certain roads, &c, on very thin paper. A map of the Lake Nicaragua, one sheet, manuscript. Two maps on common paper, and coarsely executed, very long and narrow; one of the river Chattahoochie, the other of a route from Washington City to Mobile. A map of part of New Orleans territory and

Florida, manuscripts, thin paper. Let all these be rolled up in one roll, and on a round stick. The widest first, and so on. These, with anything else you may have to forward to me, must be put into the hands of Mrs. Stoker, at J. Bentham's house, Queen Square Place, Westminster, by nine o'clock on Monday morning. This lady is Mr. Bentham's housekeeper. Ask at 30 Craven Street for letters for me."

Burr explains to Swartout that Spanish Florida, which at this time stretches from the Atlantic to the Mississippi, is ripe for the picking. "It is a country very thinly peopled, there being not more than 2500 families in the whole extent of six hundred miles, from St. Augustine to Baton Rouge. The American settlement (above the Spanish line) on the Mobile is about 400 families, and dependent wholly on the towns of Mobile and Pensacola, having no other course to market but down the Mobile. The Natchez settlement, just above the line, and bordering on the Mississippi, is flourishing and wealthy, and, if you can get access to it, will take all your merchandise, and supply as much cotton as you may be disposed to purchase. The persons whose names I have given you will put you in the way to accomplish everything that may be practicable, and will aid you in the execution. The two excellencies to whom you have letters are to be approached with caution. Colonel M. and Dr. W. will advise you. Perhaps it may be expedient, in the first instance, to sound them as a merchant, without disclosing yourself further. One cannot conjecture the sort of influence which the late political changes may have had on their minds. The country over-flows with the productions you want."

What he proposes is not illegal under English law, but he has to remain cautious. Jefferson's reach is long, as an associate reminds him: "The political and personal ene-mies of Colonel Burr might not look on the Atlantic as an obstacle to their persecution, but endeavour surreptitiously to obtain, even on this side the water, communications certainly confidential, probably in their nature important."

Theo, as ever, cheers him on. When he explains that complications have required him to drop Mexico from his planning, she registers disappointment and encour-agement together. She has conceived of Mexico, a large country with great resources, as a proper field for his incomparable talents. "This certainly was inevitable," she says of his decision, "but I cannot part with what has so long lain near my heart, and not feel some regret, some sorrow. No doubt there are many other roads to happi-ness, but this appeared so perfectly suitable to you, so complete a remuneration for all the past; it so entirely coincided with my wishes relative to you, that I cherished it as my comfort, even when illness scarcely allowed me any hope of witnessing its completion." She knows, how-ever, that he will discover other outlets for his gifts. "You will not remain idle. . . . Your mind needs no external impetus. I presume that when you last wrote to me, none of your plans could be matured; but, as soon as you have formed any determinations, I conjure you to inform me of them as soon as possible. . . . My mind is anxious, impatiently anxious in regard to your future destiny. Where you are going, what will occupy you, how this will terminate, employ me continually. . . . Tell me that you are engaged in some pursuit worthy of you. This is the subject which interests me most."

32

Her reference to illness is what he notices. Her low-grade infection persists, sapping her strength. Her doctors in South Carolina puzzle over her condition; the physicians she has visited in New York on her trips there have prescribed treatment that produces temporary relief but no cure.

Burr seeks help in England. "I have taken the best medical advice which can be had in this city, and no part of the world affords so good," he writes to Joseph Alston. The most distinguished practitioner on conditions like Theo's—a Dr. Lettsome—says she must come to Britain. "He unites with me in the opinion that the only chance of saving her is a sea voyage, and a total and immediate change of climate and of habit," Burr tells Alston. "He advises a voyage to England. Something may undoubtedly be hoped from the voyage; much from the climate, to which no part of the United States can bear any comparison; and still more, perhaps, from the enlightened and experienced medical aid which is found here. Dr. Lettsome has performed wonderful cures in analogous cases;

the accounts of some of which I have read, and there is, I believe, no man in Europe who inspires so much confidence in female complaints." Theo will find equal care in no other place. "He promises to unite parental interest and tenderness with his medical skill. I propose to unite with him Dr. Bailey, a man of genius, of profound learning, and of vigorous and intuitive mind. With such aid, and under my direction and control, we may justly hope for all that human means can effect."

Burr explains to Alston that he has arranged everything his wife will need for the trip. "I have provided for her reception at every port at which she may probably land, and on her arrival here she will be assured of every friendly attention from the mother of Sir George Prevost, and from two other ladies whom I have named to her. In case of any accident to me, she will find a father in that venerable sage and philosopher Jeremy Bentham, of whose literary works you have so often heard me speak with enthusiastic admiration. He is, indeed, the most perfect model that I have seen or imagined of moral and intellectual excellence." Little Aaron, of course, will accompany his mother and receive similarly superlative attention. "The boy will be educated with the children of General Bentham, brother of the other, and who are incomparably the best educated children I have ever seen, as regards both their talents and their acquirements."

Burr understands that Alston requires convincing. To send his wife and son across the ocean is no trivial thing. "If there can arise in your mind objections not already removed, they must be, first, the season of the year; second, pecuniary means," Burr continues. He addresses these objections in turn. "It is true that the season does not promise a pleasant passage, but then, which is more important, it ensures a short one. The dangers of the sea are nothing. The packets are such stanch ships and so well found, that for the last five-and-twenty years there is but a single example of one being lost, and that by an accident which will not probably occur in fifty centuries."

"As to money," Burr goes on, "I have transferred over to Theodosia the small sum which had been destined for my own expenses (say four or five hundred guineas); this will pay her passage and expenses to this place, and maintain her in the way I propose she shall live for four or five months." By then her cure should be complete.

Burr explains that he has done all he can. "I have now discharged my duty," he tells Alston. "It remains for you to fulfill yours."

He makes his case to Theo. "In advising you to come here, I have endeavoured to take a view of everything connected with the subject," he says. "You will, nevertheless, act your discretion. But it is my belief that there is no other chance of your recovery, and I have a strong persuasion that before you were here two months you would be well. It will be a dull day to me on which I shall hear that you are not coming. Yet I repeat that it is you who must finally decide."

In fact, it is events that decide the matter. "The embargo is not yet raised, nor is there any probability that it will," she replies. War with Britain, the bête noire of the Republicans, looms. Theo risks being stranded in Europe. "I have been seriously told that it would not be in my power to return home by water, because our coasts would soon be lined with English cruisers. . . . A voyage to join you at any season, and through any danger, would be a most delightful party of pleasure to me; but it is now impracticable."

She knows he will be disappointed, so she adds a heartening note: "Console yourself with the most unanswerable objection to this voyage—my health is better. Relief has not yet been obtained, but my strength, spirits and appearance I have very much regained, and I trust that nature will soon effect the rest." Yet she can't resist chiding him: "You should not have tantalized me with this proposed voyage. It is quite out of my reach."

33

The news that she won't be coming discourages him. So does the lack of response to his western schemes. The British government, on the verge of war with the United States over the seizure of American vessels and other real and perceived insults, will countenance nothing that threatens Spain, an ally. Nor does it want to give the American government, about to be headed by James Madison as Jefferson's successor, cause for war until Britain is fully ready. The British government warns off Burr's potential collaborators, leaving him bereft. "In my state of nullity I wish to be forgotten till I can rise to view in a shape worthy of the hopes of my friends," he writes morosely in January 1809.

He diverts himself with a journey to Scotland. "The time passed at Edinburgh was a continued round of dissipation, dinners, suppers, balls, routs," he records in a journal he will share with Theo. "Edinburgh is the most hospitable and social place I have been. They meet to amuse and be amused, and they succeed. The Scotch women dance much better than the English, if I may be allowed to judge from the samples which I have seen of the latter. It is in the reel (the Scotch reel) that the lassies are seen to best advantage; their animation and activity exceeding anything that you can imagine—a reel after supper. They bound, spring, twirl, raise their hands, snap the fingers—yet with grace."

He returns to England only to be told he must leave again. "My presence in this country was thought embarrassing to his majesty's government," he writes. He contests the deportation order by the novel strategy, for a Revolutionary War veteran and a former vice president of the United States, of claiming to be a British subject. He points out that the British crown denies the right of alienation; once a British subject, the government holds, always a British subject. He was born a British subject, he observes, and therefore still is a British subject, or ought to be by London's lights. The argument draws smiles from those who hear it but no assent from the responsible ministries. A foreign alien, he must go.

But go where? Few countries to which the British are willing to send him are willing to allow him entry. "The government would agree to no place but Heligoland, a barren island about sixty miles from the coast of Denmark, now in possession of Great Britain," he writes Theo. At the last minute, fortune, in the shape of the Swedish minister, steps in and grants him a passport to Sweden.

He finds the Swedes to be a striking people, with curious ways. The women are stunning; he writes appreciatively of finding himself amid "a galaxy of Swedish beauty," and adds: "I have nowhere seen a greater proportion than

at Stockholm." The people are as honest as the Scandina-
vian summer days are long. "It is impossible not to love
and admire the character of this people," he tells Theo.
"Honesty is not a virtue here; it is a mere habit. Coming
from England, where no vigilance can secure you against
fraud and theft, it is like passing to another planet to travel
in this, where you sleep in security without a latch to your
door; where you may send your trunk, without a lock, to
any distance, without hazard, though driven by a child,
often a little girl, at all hours of night, in their little open
chairs. This circumstance, the beauty of their roads, being
everywhere like that from New York to Harlem, and the
kindness and cheerful good-humour with which you are
everywhere received, render travelling very pleasant in this
country. It is also the cheapest in the world. A horse and
chair, with driver, costs less than three cents per English
mile, and no toll."

Yet the Swedes' openness can be disconcerting. "Do
remind me to give you a dissertation on locking doors," he
writes Theo. "Every person, of every sex and grade, comes
in without knocking. Plump into your bedroom. They do
not seem at all embarrassed, nor think of apologizing at
finding you in bed, or dressing, or doing no matter what,
but go right on and tell their story as if all were right. If
the door be locked and the key outside (they use altogether
spring-locks here), no matter; they unlock the door, and
in they come. It is vain to desire them to knock; they do
not comprehend you, and, if they do, pay no manner of
attention to it. It took me six weeks to teach my old Anna
not to come in without knocking; and, finally, it was only

by appearing to get into a most violent passion, and threatening to blow out her brains, which she had not the least doubt I would do without ceremony. I engage she is the only servant in all Sweden who ever knocks. Notwithstanding all my caution, I have been almost every day disturbed in this way, and once last week was surprised in the most awkward situation imaginable. So, madam, when you come to Svenska, remember to lock the door and to take the key inside."

He boasts of Theo to his hosts. "Good God!" replies one distinguished interlocutor, a portrait painter to whom he has shown Theo's image. "Pardon the freedom, but can any man on earth be worthy of that woman? I know how to estimate her. Such a union of delicacy, dignity, sweetness and genius I never saw. . . . Is she happy?" Burr adds: "He almost shed tears."

He grumbles at not hearing from her, or anyone else. "Called at the post office. No letters. No doubt my letters are stopped by the British government. 'Tis impossible that every human being can have forgotten me for four months; for my female friends, I would swear. But what remedy? *Me voici.*"

He contracts a fever. "On getting home at eight, found all my maladies exceedingly increased," he tells Theo. "A very quick pulse, agitation of nerves, and burning hot, though the weather is quite cold, and I had drank very little wine." He medicates himself. "Ordered hot water and warm drink, but no relief; though lay in bed, exceedingly restless. Took thirteen drops of laudanum, the greatest dose I ever took; and, finding sleep quite out of the question, got up, dressed and read a long, dull *comedie*. . . . About two a.m. a little relieved. Went to bed; slept about four hours and got up well. There prevails in this city a malignant fever, which has carried off persons in two and three days. Having been often in the quarter most infected with this disease, no doubt I had caught it, and I have given you this detail to show how very slightly any such disease can affect me. I disclosed to no one that I was sick. A sick man is a very contemptible animal."

When a letter from Theo finally arrives, he devours every word. "My boy continues devotedly attached to you," she says. "His education advances. He reads and speaks French with facility. Reads English well, and begins with Latin this day." She exudes love and admiration for her distant father. "I witness your extraordinary fortitude with new wonder at every new misfortune. Often, after reflecting on this subject, you appear to me so superior, so elevated above all other men; I contemplate you with such a strange mixture of humility, admiration, reverence, love and pride, that very little superstition would be necessary to make me worship you as a superior being: such enthusiasm does your character excite in me. When I afterward revert to myself, how insignificant do my best qualities appear. My vanity would be greater if I had not been placed so near you; and yet my pride is our relationship. I had rather not live than not be the daughter of such a man."

34

He ventures to France in the spring of 1810, on the premise
that if the British won't support his project, perhaps their
mortal enemies will. But Napoleon and his ministers
decide that with Britain and the United States on the
brink of war, France should do nothing to upset the American government and divert American enmity from Britain. Burr finds himself stranded in Paris with neither
prospects nor income. At first he economizes for the sake
of Theo and Aaron. "I never spend a livre that I do not
calculate what pretty thing it might have bought for you
and Gampillo," he writes Theo, employing one of his pet
names for his grandson (and alternatively for himself).
"Hence my economy." Gradually, though, economy is
required for his own sake. He makes light of it. "Did not
take my coffee blanc this evening, having no coal; so consoled myself with milk punch. My uncle Stephen lived on
milk punch, and, at the age of eighty-six, mounted by the
stirrup a very gay horse, and galloped off with me twelve
miles without stopping, and was, I thought, less fatigued
than I." A few weeks later: "I allow myself sugar; but,

madame, I have dismissed my barber, which is a saving of at least fifteen livres per month." By October he denies himself heat. "The mornings are already so cold that I shudder at the thoughts of getting out of bed." He consumes whatever costs least. "Ate a pound of grapes"—it being the harvest season. For a time he rationalizes his one luxury: "Though a man may be a little the poorer for drinking good wine, yet he is, under its influence, much more able to bear poverty." But then even this has to go, and he is reduced to the cheapest *vin de table*, with predictable results: "It made me sick and stupid." The weather grows chillier and so does he. "Home; very cold, and no fire." He nears naked destitution. "My boots are at the shoemaker's to be soled. They are done, and I cannot redeem them." His usual bonhomie begins to flag. "My affairs are quite stagnant, and I have no other prospect but that of starving in Paris."

He tries to leave France, but the French government won't let him depart. "Fair promises and civil words have been received, but nothing more," he tells Theo. He learns that a land scheme in which he has invested comes close to fruition but will finally mature only with his presence in Holland. "If I now had a passport to go to Amsterdam, I would clear for myself ten thousand dollars in a fortnight." But the passport remains beyond his reach. "Verily, I shall starve."

He borrows money to pay for food he has already eaten and finds himself as hungry as ever. His penury distracts him, and his distraction nearly lands him in jail. "Rain, snow, and hard wind. . . . Deliberating on the state of my finances, found that this *sans sous* state was not only inconvenient but dangerous; for instance this morning I hit a glass window with my umbrella, and had nearly forced it through one of those large panes. In such a case you have only to pay, and there's an end of it; but, had I broken the pane and not been able to pay for it, I must, infallibly, have been taken before a *commissaire de police* to abide his judgment." He resorts to extreme measures. "Casting about for ways and means, not one occurred to me but that of robbing poor little Gampy. I opened his little treasure of coins and medals to see what could be spared, and finally seized one Danish dollar (thaler) of Charles VII and two Swedish thalers of Gustav IV. With these I went off to a changeur, who gave me five francs five sous each." The wolf remains outside the door, but barely. "Yesterday was cold, and today colder," he writes on the last day of 1810. "Quite winter. The gutters all froze hard. Put on my flannel waistcoat this morning, as I wear no surtout, for a great many philosophical reasons; principally because I have not got one."

He scrounges an offer of work. "I am about to undertake the translation from English into French of two octavo volumes for one hundred louis," he reports to Theo. "It will take me three months hard work. Better than to starve. But the most curious part of the story is that the book in question contains a quantity of abuse and libels on A. Burr."

35

Theo receives his letters belatedly and imperfectly. He switches ciphers to frustrate American agents and authorities but neglects, in his now-constant struggle to find enough to eat, to send her the new key. "I have worked, and wept, and torn the paper," she replies, "and thrown myself down in despair, and rose full of some new thought, and tried again to fail again, till my heart is worn out with a constant renewal of the same scene. Still, however, all your last letters remained unciphered. I continue to make some new attempt now almost daily, but in vain. . . . I beseech you, resume the old cipher, or in that send me the new key."

She writes on his behalf to his former friends. "I venture to address you on a subject which it is almost dangerous to mention, and which, in itself, affords me no claim on your attention," she explains to Albert Gallatin, who as Treasury secretary knows the mind of the Madison administration. "I venture to inquire whether you suppose that my father's return to this country would be productive of ill consequences to him, or draw on him farther prosecution from any branch of the government." She asks Gallatin to consider her position and her father's. "Recollect what are my incitements. Recollect that I have seen my father dashed from the high rank he held in the minds of his countrymen, imprisoned and forced into exile. Must he ever remain thus excommunicated from the participation of domestic enjoyments and the privileges of a citizen, aloof from his accustomed sphere and singled out as a mark for the shafts of calumny? Why should he be thus proscribed and held up in execration? What benefit to the country can possibly accrue from the continuation of this system? Surely it must be evident to the worst enemies of my father that no man situated as he will be could obtain any undue influence, even supposing him desirous of it."

Gallatin responds equivocally, and Theo takes equivocation, after the years of Republican persecution, as a positive sign. She calls on her father to return home. "I say *come;* land in New York." She would prefer to bring him to South Carolina, but she believes he must go first to the site of his original troubles, to which place he must repair eventually. "Nothing can be done here. Your arrival will be known. The news of it will reach New York long before you. The fervency of surprise and delighted friendship will have time to cool, cabals to be formed, and measures to be taken." No, he must return directly to the city from which he fled. "Go to New York. Make your stand there. . . . Civil debts may be procrastinated, for a time, by confinement to the limits. There you can take breath; openly see your friends; make your arrangements; and soon, I think, you will be able to throw off those momentary shackles, and resume your station."

She knows she is asking him to abandon much of what he has dreamed of and worked for during the past decade. But the dream of empire is gone already, at least for him. His enemies are too numerous and powerful. He must acknowledge defeat and come home.

36

Her plea breaks his heart and then his will. For her he has schemed and struggled—for her and his grandson, to leave them a name and a feeling of family accomplishment. In his poverty and distress he has rarely missed a day writing her, if only in his journal. He still goes without a fire and without eating to save some coins for the boy: souvenirs of the adventure he will relate to him personally someday.

But he bows to her plea and to the inevitable. He applies again for a passport. And again. And again. He appeals to friends to intercede on his behalf. Months go by; the French bureaucracy moves glacially, infuriatingly. Hope gleams, then disappears. "A deadly blow," he writes after one flicker is extinguished. Spring comes to Paris, easing the pinch of winter's cold. Summer follows, bringing heat and new fevers to one whose health has already been compromised.

A duke takes his part. The blockade is broken. The passport is imminent, he is told. He refuses to believe it. "I shall not feel great confidence till I have the thing in my hand," he writes Theo.

A note from the duke himself: the passport has been issued, circumspectly under another false name: Adolphus Arnot. "Now, indeed, I may hope," Burr writes Theo. "Now I feel as if I was embracing you and Gamp."

He exits France via Holland. His cash is gone; to underwrite his Atlantic passage he must sell his remaining personal property, including a watch he has purchased for Theo and which he has carried across Europe, thinking of her. "After turning it over, and looking at it, and opening it, and putting it to my ear like a baby, and kissing it, and begging you a thousand pardons out loud, your dear, little, beautiful watch was—was sold. . . . If my clothes had been saleable, they would have gone first, that's sure." But he won't dwell on his loss, if it brings him closer to her. "Heigho! When I get rich I will buy you a prettier one." The next breath reveals his mingled emotions. "I feel as if I were already on the way to you, and my heart beats with joy. Yet, alas! that country which I am so anxious to revisit will perhaps reject me with horror."

Still further hindrances emerge, these the result of Britain's blockade of France and its allies. "I forget that the little island of Great Britain lies between us, and, what is worse, their ships; there are now four of them in full sight not two leagues off. But, as we have neither merchandise nor Frenchmen on board, I think they will let us go."

They finally do let the ship go but only to England, where the vessel, an American craft, is seized by the government. Delays mount upon delays, stretching weeks and then months. He dodges old friends, even Jeremy Bentham, lest they see him in his reduced state. He survives by selling books, clothes and other items he left behind on departing Britain. The new year, 1812, finds him still in Britain and finds Britain and America closer to war. "If there be war before April, every American ship which shall sail, even from this day, will be captured," he writes Theo. "Indeed, my dear *enfans*, Gampillo"—Burr himself this time—"had never so bad a prospect of seeing you."

Finally, with borrowed bribes, he arranges passage aboard another ship and at the end of March gets away. "I shake the dust off my feet," he records in his journal. "Adieu, John Bull! *Insula inhospitabilis*, as you were truly called 1800 years ago."

But now the wind and sea rise against him; a late-winter gale drives the vessel backward. The captain maneuvers among icebergs propelled by the wind and currents. "If a ship going at six or seven knots should come in contact with one of them, the shock would certainly be fatal," he observes phlegmatically.

The vessel at last makes land at Boston in early May. He has to clear customs but discovers that the collector is the son of a political enemy. "For me to go direct to him to take an oath and demand a permit in the name of Arnot seemed to be an experiment that promised little success, and in the case of discovery might expose me to serious inconveniences," he writes Theo. But to travel to the next customhouse, at Newburyport, will cost money he doesn't have. He determines to take the chance. Among the crowd of passengers he slips past his enemy's son.

He lies quietly at Boston awaiting a packet to New

York. When one appears he bluffs his way aboard, still posing as Arnot. His heart clutches when he hears his real name: "Ah, Burr! How goes it?" He glances cautiously toward the speaker and is greatly relieved to see that another man is being addressed, the captain's brother, who apparently has the given name Burr.

The boat proceeds south and west until the wind dies off Long Island, leaving the sails slack and the passengers to languish almost within sight of their destination. But finally Burr passes through the narrows at the entrance to New York's harbor.

Still he is not quite home. The tide turns and the wind fails, leaving the boat within sight of Manhattan but not within reach. Burr jumps ship onto a smaller craft, which becomes similarly stranded. He hails a still smaller boat whose rowers accept a dollar to put him ashore.

He looks up one of his few remaining friends. But the man is not at his Water Street home. Burr spends the night on the floor of a dingy rooming house. In the morning he returns to Water Street and discovers, to his great relief, that his friend is back.

"And here I am," he writes Theo from his friend's brother's house. It has been four years since they parted.

37

He remains in hiding till he hears from Theo. His ambitions have turned to dust, his fame to a noose about his neck. For her alone, and for young Aaron, does he live. To see them will repay his foreign hardships and the hazards of his return from exile.

The first news of his daughter and grandson comes in a letter from Joseph Alston. The opening sentence bodes ill. "A few miserable weeks since, my dear sir . . . ," Alston says, "I would have congratulated you on your return in the language of happiness. With my wife on one side and my boy on the other, I felt myself superior to depression. The present was enjoyed, the future was anticipated with enthusiasm."

But malign fate has intervened. "One dreadful blow has destroyed us; reduced us to the veriest, the most sublimated wretchedness. That boy, on whom all rested; our companion, our friend—he who was to have transmitted down the mingled blood of Theodosia and myself—he who was to have redeemed all your glory, and shed new lustre upon our families—that boy, at once our happiness and our pride, is taken from us—*is dead*."

Alston doesn't say how Aaron died; Burr supposes a sudden fever. Alston explains that he and Theo are beside themselves with grief, but they are determined to carry on. "My own hand surrendered him to the grave, yet we are alive. . . . I will not conceal from you that life is a burden, which, heavy as it is, we shall both support, if not with dignity, at least with decency and firmness. Theodosia has endured all that a human being could endure, but her admirable mind will triumph. She supports herself in a manner worthy of your daughter."

Through the darkness shines one thin beam, at least for Burr. "My present wish is that Theodosia should join you, with or without me, as soon as possible," Alston says. "I not only recognise your claim to her after such a separation, but change of scene and your society will aid her, I am conscious, in recovering at least that tone of mind which we are destined to carry through life with us."

Theo herself writes. "Alas! my dear father, I do live, but how does it happen? Of what am I formed that I live, and why? Of what service can I be in this world, either to you or anyone else? . . . Whichever way I turn, the same anguish still assails me. . . . I think Omnipotence could give me no equivalent for my boy; no, none—none."

She looks to her father for consolation. "I wish to see you, and will leave as soon as possible." But she can't leave right away. "I could not go alone by land, for our coachman is a great drunkard, and requires the presence of a master; and my husband is obliged to wait for a military court of inquiry." Alston commands a brigade in the South Carolina militia and must attend the court's session. "It will sit on the 10th of August. How long it will be in session I know not. After that we shall set off, though I do not perceive how it is possible to speak with certainty. . . . When we do go, he thinks of going by water, but is not determined. It will probably be late in August before we go. God bless you, my beloved father. Write to me sometimes."

Burr has often said that he and Theo must support each other in their trials. She can't see what support she will be for him now. "I am not insensible to your affection, nor quite unworthy of it, though I can offer nothing in return but the love of a broken, deadened heart, still desirous of promoting your happiness, if possible. God bless you."

38

Burr, stricken at the loss of his grandson, holds to the hope of his daughter's coming. But the business of the Carolina military court, followed by the long-expected outbreak of war with Britain, detains Alston for weeks, then months. Theo grows impatient yet remains at his side. Burr's days drag; he feels in exile still, unable to see the one he loves.

South Carolina's business claims Alston longer. His friends urge him to run for governor, saying the moment is ripe and mustn't be missed. He heeds their advice and wins. He tells Theo he doesn't know when he'll be able to leave the state.

Burr resigns himself to waiting. He cautiously resumes his life in New York and gradually discovers, to his relief, that politics has forgotten him. His enemies are retired, dead or sufficiently powerful to feel unthreatened by his return. A few old friends help him financially; one lends him the use of his law library so he can reconstruct his law practice.

But he spends most of his time looking figuratively to sea, awaiting the news that Theo is coming. As winter approaches, with no indication that Alston will be able to escape his obligations, Burr sends a man to accompany his daughter north. To the ordinary hazards of sea travel are now added the special dangers of war. "I have engaged a passage to New York for your daughter in a pilot-boat that has been out privateering," Burr's man writes him a few days before Christmas, referring to the American practice of licensing private vessels to act as wartime raiders. "My only fears are that Governor Alston may think the mode of conveyance too undignified, and object to it; but Mrs. Alston is fully bent on going. . . . We shall sail in about eight days."

39

Burr joyfully marks his calendar. His exile from his darling is finally to end. The pilot boat, the *Patriot*, is a fast schooner; with fair winds it will make the passage from South Carolina in less than a week.

As the blessed day approaches he frequents the waterfront, scanning the lower Hudson for a pilot boat, assessing every schooner, asking the watermen what they've heard of British depredations against American vessels. Each evening he returns to his modest quarters, believing the boat's failure to arrive simply increases its chances of appearing the next day.

But day after day yields the same result. Nothing is seen of Theo's boat, nothing heard. Burr tries to force back the fear that presses toward his mind and heart. Revelers celebrate Twelfth Night, but the worried father can't join them. January's second week slips by, and still no sign of his daughter. He has traveled enough to know that winds fail and vessels are becalmed; surely her boat will arrive soon. He learns of a storm off Cape Hatteras; perhaps the *Patriot* found a harbor and waited out the tempest.

Another week passes, then still another. He grows frantic. The overland mail brings a letter from Alston to Theo, posted at Columbia, South Carolina, and dated January 15. Burr holds the letter, unopened. A second letter, to him, arrives several days later. "Tomorrow will be three weeks since, in obedience to your wishes, Theodosia left me," Alston writes. "It is three weeks, and not yet one line from her. My mind is tortured. . . . The three weeks without a letter fill me with an unhappiness—a wretchedness I can neither describe nor conquer." Alston writes what Burr hasn't let himself contemplate. "Gracious God! Is my wife, too, taken from me?"

Another week, another letter. "I parted with our Theo near the bar about noon on Thursday, the last of December," Alston explains. "The wind was moderate and fair. . . . From that moment I have heard nothing of the schooner nor my wife. I have been the prey of feelings which you only can imagine. When I turned from the grave of my boy I deemed myself no longer vulnerable; misfortune had no more a blow for me. I was wrong. It is true, I no longer feel, I never shall feel as I was wont; but I have been taught that there was still one being in whom I was inexpressibly interested."

And now that one being has vanished. "I have in vain endeavoured to build upon the hope of long passage. Thirty days are decisive. My wife is either captured or lost."

Yet this ambiguity offers its own slight hope. "A short time since, and the idea of capture would have been the source of painful, terrible apprehension," Alston says. "It now furnishes me the only ray of comfort, or rather of hope, that I have." If the capture was by the British, Theo is alive, although a winter voyage aboard a man-of-war will test her troubled health. If the capture was by pirates, who have long plagued that treacherous coast, the chances are less but more than nil; the pirates might hold her for ransom.

But either way, Alston or Burr should have heard something. Or one of them would hear something soon. "Each mail is anticipated with impatient, yet fearful and appalling anxiety," Alston says. He needn't add, but does so anyway: "Should you hear aught relative to the object of this our common solicitude, do not, I pray, forget me."

Burr continues to walk the waterfront. His step sometimes falters but never fails. He scrutinizes every mail. For weeks, nothing. Nothing from the British navy, nothing from kidnappers seeking a ransom. Nothing even from Alston.

Finally Alston writes again. Burr reads the letter, an admission of defeat and tragic loss, a full two months after Theo was due. "This, then, is the end of all the hopes we had formed," Alston says. "Oh, my friend, if there be such a thing as the sublime of misery, it is for us that it has been reserved. You are the only person in the world with whom I can commune on this subject; for you are the only person whose feelings can have any community with mine. You knew those we loved. With you, therefore, it will be no weakness to feel their loss." Alston's friends have tried to fathom what her disappearance means. "They seem to consider it like the loss of an ordinary woman. Alas! they know nothing of my heart. They never have known anything of it. . . . But the man who has been deemed worthy of the heart of *Theodosia Burr*, and who has felt what it was to be blessed with such a woman's, will never forget his elevation."

40

Burr falls silent. There is nothing to say. His few friends seek to console him; even his enemies nod to him on the street, affirming a human bond deeper than politics and acknowledging a loss more profound than most, thank God, must suffer.

He seeks solace in the law. He displays the skill he has always possessed. But his energy is gone. Without Theo to inspire him, he cannot dream.

The years pass. He watches with curiosity but neither self-justification nor bitterness as Andrew Jackson is acclaimed a hero for irregularly forcing the Spanish from Florida, as he himself proposed to do. He quietly applauds Mexico for attaining the independence he had sought for her. He sees a new country carved out of Mexico, with Sam Houston and his Texas comrades accomplishing much of what he had envisioned decades earlier.

He fades into history and inconsequence, almost forgotten . . .

41

"*I was traveling up the Hudson on board of a steam boat,*"
a journalist records a dozen years after Theo's disappearance. "It was a delightful afternoon in summer; the sky
was serene, and the sweet balmy zephyrs played upon the
face of the tranquil river. . . . The company on board con-
sisted of a gay and fashionable assemblage of both sexes,
whose sprightly conversation contributed to heighten the
interest of the scene."

The journalist examined the passengers more closely.
"My attention was arrested by the singular appearance of
a grave, elderly gentleman, whom I observed sitting on
one of the side seats, apparently absorbed in some pensive
musings, with his eyes fixed on the rolling tide. There was
a melancholy dignity in his countenance; his venerable
locks, gray with age, hung loosely on his shoulders. His
dress was a coat considerably worn and short breeches,
after the old fashion." To outward appearances the man
might have been a country farmer, returning home after a
visit to the city. "Little attention was, therefore, paid by
those pert fashionables, to one whom they considered an

unlettered rustic. . . . Indeed, the old gentleman's taciturnity, and the antiquity of his dress, afforded no small amusement to some merry wags—a kind of buffoons with whom we meet in almost every mixed company."

The discussion grew more animated. "It happened that some gentlemen who belonged to the bar, had commenced a controversy on some critical point in law, very near the old gentleman. He occasionally regarded them with a look, as if to penetrate the recesses of their souls; and then resumed his posture. At length, a young smart, with a significant glance, accosted him: 'Old gentleman, what is your opinion?'

"The man of silence and mystery spoke—and lo! what was our astonishment! His countenance, which was before shaded with the gloom of melancholy, brightened with intelligence; the loftiest eloquence flowed from his tongue, which was so long silent; and those eyes which were vacantly fixed upon the passing wave, now beamed with the fire of his soul! The transcendent brightness of his mind now broke forth—the halo of genius shone around him. The disputants viewed him with silent wonder. The importance of the sons and daughters of fashion vanished like mist before the rising sun. All eyes were fixed upon the extraordinary stranger—all were desirous to know his name.

"Inquiry was made—and, reader! that stranger was AARON BURR!"

SOURCES

The principal source for the present book is the correspondence between Aaron Burr and Theodosia Burr
Alston. Surviving letters between the two appear primarily in *Memoirs of Aaron Burr, with Miscellaneous Selections
from His Correspondence*, edited by Matthew L. Davis, two
volumes (1836); and *Correspondence of Aaron Burr and His
Daughter Theodosia*, edited by Mark Van Doren (1929).
*The Private Journal of Aaron Burr During His Residence of
Four Years in Europe, With Selections from His Correspondence*, edited by Matthew L. Davis, two volumes (1838),
covers the exile years. The *Memoirs* contain letters from
Aaron Burr to many other correspondents, as do the *Papers
of Aaron Burr*, twenty-seven reels of microfilm (1977), and
Political Correspondence and Public Papers of Aaron Burr,
edited by Mary-Jo Kline, two volumes (1983). *Trial of
Aaron Burr for Treason, Printed from the Report Taken in
Short Hand*, edited by David Robertson, two volumes
(1875), reproduces arguments and testimony from the
1807 trial.

Aaron Burr has been the subject of many biographies,

of which the serious ones began with James Parton's *The Life and Times of Aaron Burr* (1857) and continue through Nancy Isenberg's *Fallen Founder: The Life of Aaron Burr* (2007). Thomas Fleming's *Duel: Alexander Hamilton, Aaron Burr, and the Future of America* (1999) is the most revealing recent telling of the fateful encounter at Weehawken.

Theodosia Burr Alston has received much less attention than her father. Charles F. Pidgin's *Theodosia: The First Gentlewoman of Her Time* (1907) and Richard Côté's *Theodosia Burr Alston: Portrait of a Prodigy* (2003) are the most thorough biographies in a small field.

The events and individuals surrounding Burr and Theo are the subject of many hundreds of worthy volumes, for they constitute the story of America during the late eighteenth and early nineteenth centuries.